compiled by LEXUS *with Lesley Robertson*

FAST A-Z REFERENCE GRAMMAR
FOR EXAMS AND SELF STUDY

Chambers

First published 1983 by Richard Drew Publishing Ltd
Second edition 1988

This edition published 1991 by W & R Chambers Ltd,
43–45 Annandale Street, Edinburgh EH7 4AZ

© Chambers and Lexus Ltd 1983

All rights reserved. No part of this publication may be
reproduced, stored in a retrieval system, or transmitted, in
any form or by any means, electronic, mechanical,
photocopying, recording or otherwise, without the prior
permission of W & R Chambers Ltd.

British Library Cataloguing in Publication Data

A catalogue record for this book is
available from the British Library

ISBN 0-550-22060-7

Cover illustration by Michael Dancer
Cover design by Grafik Design Works

Printed and bound in Great Britain by Cox & Wyman Ltd

YOUR SCHOOLMATE

gives you all the basic facts you need to know for learning French and checking up grammar. In one single, easy-to-use A-Z list your French SCHOOLMATE tells you all about:

* basic grammatical facts with clear explanations and useful tables
* French verbs – with models, irregular forms and use of tenses
* the main uses of key words such as 'avoir', 'dont', 'en', 'faire' etc
* numbers, the calendar and how to tell the time
* pronunciation – how to pronounce French and how to relate the spelling of a word to its sound

YOUR SCHOOLMATE

makes learning easier for you, since it gives you everything in one A-Z list. So if you want to check up on gender in French, you just look up under 'gender' in the proper alphabetical order. And if you are not sure about the names of grammatical categories – like 'personal pronouns' or 'possessives' – you will find a cross-reference under the entries for 'mon', 'lui' etc. Whenever a word is written in CAPITAL LETTERS this means you'll find more information under that entry. Reference is easy – and fast.

YOUR SCHOOLMATE is ideal for:

✓ language learning
✓ exam revision
✓ self-study
✓ fast reference
✓ getting things right

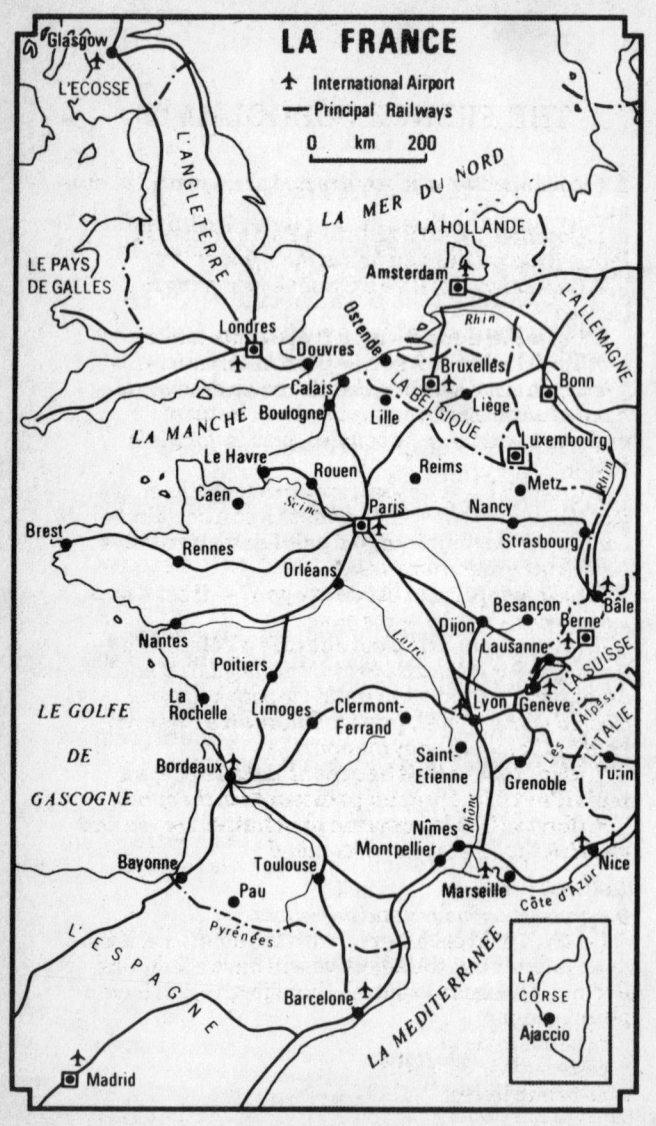

THE FRENCH SCHOOLMATE

à (combined with 'le': contracted as **au**; with 'les' as **aux**)

1. (*location: in, at*) **il habite à Paris** *he lives in Paris;* **il est au bureau** *he's at the office*

2. (*movement: to*) **il va à Genève** *he's going to Geneva*

3. (*to*) **je l'ai donné à mon frère** *I gave it to my brother;* **il l'a lancé à son copain** *he threw it to his friend;* **ils ont distribué des livres aux élèves** *they handed out books to the pupils;* **il a acheté un cadeau à son frère** *he bought a present for his brother*

4. (*from*) **il l'a acheté au supermarché** *he bought it at the supermarket;* **il l'a acheté à son copain** *he bought it from his friend;* **il a pris l'eau au robinet** *he took the water from the tap*

5. (*belonging*) **à qui est ce crayon? — il est à moi** *whose pencil is this? — it's mine*

6. (*means, manner*) **c'est chauffé à l'électricité ou au gaz?** *is it heated by electricity or gas?;* **il a fallu dégager le chemin à la pelle** *the path had to be cleared with a shovel;* **payé au mois ou à l'heure** *paid by the month or by the hour*

7. (*date, time*) **à huit heures** *at eight o'clock;* **au mois d'avril** *in April;* **au printemps** *in the spring*

8. (*farewells*) **à la semaine prochaine!** *see you next week!;* **à lundi!** *see you on Monday!*

adjectives

♦ *Agreement of nouns and adjectives*

Adjectives in French 'agree' with the noun – i.e. if the noun is feminine, the adjective will have a feminine ending; if the noun is plural, the adjective will have a plural ending:

    la petite maison
    cette maison est petite
    de beaux livres

6 ADJECTIVES

Like nouns, the regular feminine is formed by adding '-e' to the masculine unless it already ends in '-e':

MASCULINE	FEMININE
petit	petite
vert	verte
bleu	bleue
but { jeune	jeune } no change
vide	vide

The regular plural is formed by adding '-s' to the singular:

petits	petites
verts	vertes
bleus	bleues
jeunes	jeunes
vides	vides

Other feminine endings of adjectives ('semi-irregular'). The phonetic symbols in brackets are explained under PRONUNCIATION:

MASCULINE	FEMININE
(a) vif[1], neuf (vif, nœf)	vive, neuve (viv, nœv)
(b) heureux, jaloux (œRø, ʒalu)	heureuse, jalouse (œRøz, ʒaluz)
menteur[2] (mɑ̃tœR)	menteuse (mɑ̃tœz)
(c) léger (leʒe)	légère (leʒɛR)
premier (pRəmje)	première (pRəmjɛR)
(d) bas[3] (bɑ)	basse (bɑs)
cruel (kRyɛl)	cruelle (kRyɛl)
épais (epɛ)	épaisse (epɛs)
gentil (ʒɑ̃ti)	gentille (ʒɑ̃tij)
gras (gRɑ)	grasse (gRɑs)
gros (gRo)	grosse (gRos)
las (lɑ)	lasse (lɑs)
muet[4] (mɥɛ)	muette (mɥɛt)
pareil (paRɛj)	pareille (paRɛj)
sot (so)	sotte (sɔt)
(e) bon (bɔ̃)	bonne (bɔn)
italien (italjɛ̃)	italienne (italjɛn)
paysan (peizɑ̃)	paysanne (peizan)

ADJECTIVES

Exceptions:
1. bref (bʀɛf) — brève (bʀɛv)
2. meilleur (mɛjœʀ) — meilleure (mɛjœʀ)
   supérieur (sypɛʀjœʀ) — supérieure (sypɛʀjœʀ)
   inférieur (ɛ̃fɛʀjœʀ) — inférieure (ɛ̃fɛʀjœʀ)
3. ras (ʀɑ) — rase (ʀɑz)
4. complet (kɔ̃plɛ) — complète (kɔ̃plɛt)
   discret (diskʀɛ) — discrète (diskʀɛt)
   inquiet (ɛ̃kjɛ) — inquiète (ɛ̃kjɛt)
   secret (səkʀɛ) — secrète (səkʀɛt)

♦ Irregular Adjectives

MASCULINE	FEMININE
beau (bel)* (bo, bɛl)	belle (bɛl)
blanc (blɑ̃)	blanche (blɑ̃ʃ)
doux (du)	douce (dus)
faux (fo)	fausse (fos)
favori (favɔʀi)	favorite (favɔʀit)
fou (fol)* (fu, fɔl)	folle (fɔl)
frais (fʀɛ)	fraîche (fʀɛʃ)
franc (fʀɑ̃)	franche (fʀɑ̃ʃ)
long (lɔ̃)	longue (lɔ̃g)
mou (mol)* (mu, mɔl)	molle (mɔl)
nouveau (nouvel)* (nuvo, nuvɛl)	nouvelle (nuvɛl)
roux (ʀu)	rousse (ʀus)
sec (sɛk)	sèche (sɛʃ)
vieux (vieil)* (vjø, vjɛj)	vieille (vjɛj)

*The bracketed form is used before a masculine singular noun beginning with a vowel or h mute:
    un bel homme
    un fol espoir
    le nouvel an
    un vieil homme

♦ Irregular plurals of Adjectives

SINGULAR	PLURAL	EXAMPLE
-s, -x	no change	un homme heureux
		des hommes heureux
		un chapeau gris
		des chapeaux gris

8 ADJECTIVES

-eau	+x	un nouveau restaurant
		de nouveaux restaurants
-al*	-aux	un ami loyal
		des amis loyaux

*Exception: final > finals, naval > navals

◆ *Position of Adjectives*

Adjectives in French usually **follow** the noun:

du vin **rouge**** *some red wine*
un auteur **français**** *a French author*
une histoire **intéressante** *an interesting story*
un repas **délicieux** *a delicious meal*

***Adjectives of nationality/colour* **always** *follow the noun.*

Common adjectives which can come **before** the noun are:

bon (*good*); mauvais (*bad*)
vieux (*old*); jeune (*young*)
nouveau (*new*); ancien (*old*)
grand (*big*); petit (*small*)
joli (*pretty*); beau (*beautiful/handsome*)
haut (*high/tall*); long (*long*); gros (*big*)
cher (*dear*); propre (*own*); vrai (*real*)

Note however that **meaning** can vary depending on the position of these adjectives. Below are some of the most common adjectives which have one meaning when placed **before** the noun and another when placed **after**.

BEFORE NOUN

un *ancien* élève:
  a *former* pupil
un *brave* homme:
  a *good* man
un *cher* collègue:
  a *dear* colleague
ma *propre* voiture:
  my *own* car
son *vrai* nom:
  his *real* name

AFTER NOUN

un château *ancien*:
  an *old* castle
un homme *brave*:
  a *brave* man
un cadeau *cher*:
  an *expensive* present
ma voiture *propre*:
  my *clean* car
un récit *vrai*:
  a *true* account

un *grand* homme: un homme *grand*:
  a *great* man a *tall* man

♦ *Adjectives used as nouns*

quels gants préférez-vous: **les noirs** ou **les bruns?**
which gloves do you prefer – the black (ones) *or* the brown (ones)?

il y a trois maisons: **la plus petite** se trouve en face de l'église
there are three houses – the smallest *faces the church*

agreement see ADJECTIVES, GENDER, PLURALS, VERB FORMS

adverbs

Regular adverbs are formed by adding **-ment** to the feminine form of the adjective:

doucement	*gently*
franchement	*frankly*
fièrement	*proudly*

Note:

1. Adjectives ending in '-i' or '-é' in the masculine add *-ment* to the masculine form:

poliment	*politely*
délibérément	*deliberately*

2. Adjectives ending in '-ant' or '-ent' become '-amment' and '-emment'* respectively:

constant	> constamment
violent	> violemment
*Exceptions: lent	> lentement
présent	> présentement

Irregular adverbs

ADJECTIVE	ADVERB
bon (*good*)	bien (*well*)
bref (*brief*)	brièvement (*briefly*)
énorme (*enormous*)	énormément (*enormously*)
gentil (*kind*)	gentiment (*kindly*)
mauvais (*bad*)	mal (*badly*)
meilleur (*better*)	mieux (*better*)
moindre (*less*)	moins (*less*)
petit (*little*)	peu (*little*)

pire *(worse)*   pis *(worse)*
profond *(deep)*   profondément *(deeply)*

See also COMPARATIVE

aimer *(love, like; in the conditional tense: would like, prefer)*

1. j'aimerais un croissant, s'il vous plaît *I'd like a croissant, please;* **j'aimerais partir demain** *I'd like to leave tomorrow*

2. j'aimerais mieux un croissant *I'd rather have a croissant;* **j'aimerais mieux partir tout de suite** *I'd rather leave immediately*

3. j'aimerais bien aller à Paris *I'd quite like to go to Paris*

aller   for conjugation see IRREGULAR VERBS

1. *(as an auxiliary, to express immediate future: to be going to do...)* **je vais y aller tout de suite** *I'll go there immediately;* **attends — je vais répondre** *wait — I'll answer it (the phone/doorbell);* **si ça continue, je vais me fâcher** *if this goes on, I'm going to get angry;* see also VENIR

2. *(to suit, fit)* **cette veste lui va bien** *that jacket suits her; that jacket fits her;* **à huit heures, ça vous va?** *is eight o'clock all right for you?;* **cette couleur va bien avec le tapis** *that colour goes well with the carpet*

3. *(health etc)* **comment ça va?** *how are you?;* **les affaires, ça va?** *how's business?;* **ça allait mieux le mois dernier** *things were better last month;* **en Moravie maintenant ça va mal** *things aren't too good in Moravia at the moment;* **il ne va pas très bien — ils ont fait venir le docteur** *he isn't very well — they've sent for the doctor*

4. s'en aller *(to go):* **il est déjà 10 heures, on devrait s'en aller** *it's ten o'clock — we should be going;* **il s'en est allé sans rien dire** *he went off without a word;* **va-t'en!/allez-vous en!** *go away!*

après

1. *(place)* **après les feux rouges** *after the traffic lights*

2. *(time)* **après deux mois** *after two months*

3. après avoir lu le livre *after reading the book.*
4. après qu'il est parti *after he left; compare*
AVANT

articles

◆ **le, la, l'; les** — 'the' (definite article)

The French equivalent of 'the' has the four forms shown above; which one you use depends on whether the noun is masculine or feminine, singular or plural:

SINGULAR	PLURAL
le +masculine noun	
la +feminine noun	**les**
Note: **l'** +masculine/feminine noun beginning with a vowel or h mute	

Thus:

	SINGULAR	PLURAL
MASCULINE	**le** chapeau	**les** chapeaux
	le professeur	**les** professeurs
	le bureau	**les** bureaux
	l'animal	**les** animaux
	l'homme	**les** hommes
FEMININE	**la** table	**les** tables
	la voiture	**les** voitures
	la robe	**les** robes
	l'orange	**les** oranges
	l'huître	**les** huîtres

Some points to note:

1. i. after **à** (*at/to*) à+le > **au**
    à+les > **aux**

il va **au** marché *he is going to the market*
elle parle **aux** garçons/**aux** filles *she is talking to the boys/to the girls*

There is no change with 'la' or 'l'':
elle attend **à la** mairie *she is waiting at the town hall*
il est **à l'**aéroport *he is at the airport*

ii. after **de** (*of/from*) de+le > **du**
    de+les > **des**

il rentre **du** bureau *he comes back from the office*
le prix **des** gants/**des** robes *the price of the gloves/dresses*

There is no change with 'la' or 'l'':
au fond **de la** salle *at the back of the room*
vers la fin **de l'**année *towards the end of the year*

2. French uses the article 'le', 'la', 'les' where English frequently omits 'the':

   a. in generalizations:
   il n'aime pas **les** chats *he doesn't like cats*
   le vin me rend malade *wine makes me ill*

   b. with the names of most countries:
   le Canada, **la** France, **l'**Italie, **les** États-Unis

   and

   with the names of rivers:
   la Seine, **le** Rhône

Note: the article is dropped with the feminine name of a country following 'en' (*to/in*) or 'de' (*of/from*):
   il va **en** Italie
   il revient **d'**Espagne

But with the name of a country which is masculine or plural, the article combines with 'à' (*to, in*) or 'de' (*of, from*):
   il va **au** Canada
   il revient **des** Etats-Unis

   c. à **l'**université   *at/to university*
   à **l'**école   *at/to school*
   au travail   *at/to work*
   à **la** maison   *at home/home*

   d. with abstract nouns:
   la violence me dégoûte *violence disgusts me*
   elle aime **la** vie *she loves life*

   e. with price/rate:
   10F **l'**heure *10 francs an hour*
   10F **la** pièce *10 francs apiece*
   5F **le** kilo/**la** bouteille *5 francs a kilo/a bottle*
   80 km à **l'**heure *80 km an hour*

3. With parts of the body, French uses the definite article where English uses the possessive adjective 'his/her' etc:
   elle a ouvert **les** yeux *she opened her eyes*
   il marchait **les** mains dans les poches *he was walking along with his hands in his pockets*
   il a **les** cheveux courts *he has short hair/his hair is short*

◆ **un, une** — 'a' (*indefinite article*)

The French equivalent of 'a' has two forms:
   un used with a masculine singular noun
   une used with a feminine singular noun

Thus:

MASCULINE	FEMININE
un parapluie	**une** lettre
un autobus	**une** échelle
un hôpital	**une** horloge

Note: je n'ai pas **de** vélo/**d'**échelle
I haven't got a bike/a ladder

◆ **du, de la, de l'; des** — 'some'/'any' (*partitive article*)

avez-vous **du** beurre? *have you any butter?*
prenez **de la** glace *have some ice cream*
il me faut **de l'**eau *I need some water*
est-ce qu'il y a **des** pommes? *are there any apples?*
pendant **des** mois *for months*

i.e.:
du +masculine singular noun
de la+feminine singular noun
de l' +masculine/feminine noun
     beginning with a vowel or h mute
des +plural noun

Points to note:
1. Do not be influenced by the fact that 'some'/'any' can be optional in English: French *always* uses 'du', 'de la' etc:
   elle a acheté **du** lait et **des** œufs
   she bought milk and eggs

2. For the other uses of 'du', 'de la' etc see DE

3. In negative constructions the forms change to **de** (**d'** before a vowel):

	du sucre		**de** sucre
il a	**de la** glace	il n'a pas/plus *etc.*	**de** glace
il y a	**de l'**argent	il n'y a pas/ plus *etc.*	**d'**argent
	des amis		**d'**amis

Note: article retained with **ne ... que** = *only*:
elle ne boit que **de l'**eau *she only drinks water*

4. 'des' becomes 'de' before an adjective preceding the noun:
j'ai vu **de** belles maisons
I saw some beautiful houses

5. After certain constructions with 'de', the article remains **de** (**d'**):
elle a besoin **d'**eau *she needs water*
elle a besoin **de** conseils *she needs advice*

assez **1. assez de: avez-vous assez de temps/ d'assiettes?** *do you have enough time/plates?*

2. (*enough*) **tu as assez parlé** *you've spoken enough;* **je ne suis pas assez fort** *I'm not strong enough*

3. (*rather, quite*) **c'est assez difficile** *it's rather difficult;* **elle est assez jolie** *she's quite pretty*

4. j'en ai assez *I'm fed up with it*

au see A

aucun, aucune adjective or pronoun; note that there is no plural

1. aucun livre ne me plaisait *I didn't like any of the books, none of the books appealed to me;* **aucune boulangerie n'était ouverte** *there wasn't a single baker's shop open*

2. je n'en ai vu aucune qui me plaisait *I didn't see any I liked;* **il n'y en avait aucune qui allait** *not one of them was suitable*

3. aucun des deux ne marchait *neither of them*

was working; **aucun d'entre eux n'a répondu** *none of them answered*

auquel see SENTENCES

aussi 1. (*comparison*) **aussi grand que** *as big as;* **aussi peu que possible** *as little as possible*

2. (*in addition*) **prenez aussi ce livre** *take this book too;* **tu en prends, moi aussi** *you take some, and so will I;* **elle veut aller au cinéma, moi aussi** *she wants to go to the pictures, and so do I*

autant 1. **autant de: il n'avait jamais vu autant de neige** *he'd never seen so much snow;* **je n'attendais pas autant de monde** *I wasn't expecting so many people*

2. (*comparison*) **autant... que: je n'ai pas autant de livres que toi** *I don't have as many books as you;* **il gagne autant d'argent que moi** *he earns as much as I do;* **restez autant que vous voulez/voudrez** *stay as long as you like;* **il travaille toujours autant** *he is still working as hard as ever*

auxiliary see VERB FORMS

auxquels, auxquelles see SENTENCES

avant 1. (*place*) **avant les feux rouges** *before the traffic lights*

2. (*time*) **avant Noël** *before Christmas;* **avant longtemps** *before long;* **avant d'avoir lu ce livre** *before reading this book;* **avant que...: avant qu'il ait eu le temps de finir** *before he had time to finish;* **avant qu'il parte** *before he leaves;* note the use of the SUBJUNCTIVE and compare APRES

avoir as an auxiliary see VERB FORMS; for conjugation see IRREGULAR VERBS

1. (*in phrases indicating mental or physical state*) **avoir faim/soif** *to be hungry/thirsty;* **avoir peur** *to be afraid*

2. (*with measurements*) **avoir 2 mètres de long/haut** *to be 2 metres long/high*

3. (*indication of age*) **il a deux ans** *he's two (years*

old); quel âge a-t-il? *how old is he?*

4. **avoir besoin de:** j'ai besoin de ce livre *I need this book;* il n'en aura pas besoin *he won't need it*

beaucoup 1. il travaille beaucoup *he works a lot;* il ne mange pas beaucoup *he doesn't eat much;* nous ne le voyons pas beaucoup *we don't see a lot of him;* il a beaucoup travaillé *he has done a lot of work;* merci beaucoup *thank you very much;* je regrette beaucoup *I'm very sorry*

2. **beaucoup de...:** il mange beaucoup de viande *he eats a lot of meat;* il a beaucoup d'amis *he has lots of friends;* il n'y a pas beaucoup de gens qui le connaissent *not many people know him;* il y en a beaucoup *there are a lot of them;* il en a beaucoup *he has a lot (of them)*

3. c'est beaucoup trop cher *it's far too expensive;* c'est beaucoup plus loin *it's much further;* ce n'est pas beaucoup moins cher *it's not much cheaper*

bien 1. (*well*) nous avons bien travaillé *we worked well;* as-tu bien dormi? *did you sleep well?*

2. (*intensive*) tu es bien pâle *you look rather pale;* vos œufs sont-ils bien frais? *are your eggs really fresh?;* c'est bien meilleur *it's much nicer*

3. (*concessive*) **vouloir bien:** je veux bien partir maintenant *I don't mind going now;* il a bien essayé, mais... *he did try, but...*

4. **bien que...:** bien qu'il soit fatigué *although he's tired;* note the use of the SUBJUNCTIVE

5. **bien de, bien des:** bien des gens *many people;* il s'est donné bien de la peine *he took a great deal of trouble*

ça 1. (*pointing to something*) vous me donnez ça, s'il vous plaît? — non, pas ça, l'autre *give me that, will you? — no, not that one, the other one*

2. (*it, things*) ça va? *how are things?; is that ok?* ça m'étonne qu'il ne soit pas encore là *I'm surprised he hasn't arrived yet;* est-ce que ça vous dérange si je fume? *do you mind if I smoke?;* ça te va bien *it suits you*

3. oui, c'est ça *yes, that's right;* ça y est! *that's it!*

CALENDAR

calendar

♦ DAYS OF THE WEEK

(C'est) lundi   (it's) Monday
       mardi
       mercredi
       jeudi
       vendredi
       samedi
       dimanche

il arrive samedi   *he's arriving on Saturday*

il fait la grasse matinée **le samedi**   *he has a long lie on Saturdays*

jeudi matin *(on) Thursday morning*; jeudi après-midi *(on) Thursday afternoon*; jeudi soir *(on) Thursday evening*; tous les jeudis (soir) *every Thursday (evening)*; aujourd'hui/demain c'est jeudi *today's/tomorrow's Thursday*

lundi prochain/dernier   *next/last Monday*
lundi en huit/en quinze   *a week/fortnight on Monday*

♦ MONTHS

Quel jour sommes-nous? *what's today's date?*
Nous sommes le douze janvier *it's the 12th of January*
                          février
                          mars
                          avril
                          mai
                          juin
                          juillet
                          août
                          septembre
                          octobre
                          novembre
                          décembre

en mai, au mois de mai *in May*; jusqu'en avril *until April*

For all dates, except the 1st of the month, French uses cardinal numbers (i.e. 'deux', 'trois', 'quatre' etc: see NUMBERS); for the 1st, French uses 'premier':

18 CE

le cinq avril *the 5th of April*
le premier mai *the 1st of May*
le vingt-et-un mars *the 21st of March*

In letter headings, the date is often given in figures:

le 5 avril 1985
dimanche, le 7 décembre

♦ THE SEASONS

le printemps	*spring*
l'été *(m)*	*summer*
l'automne *(m)*	*autumn*
l'hiver *(m)*	*winter*

au printemps *in spring*
en été/automne/hiver *in summer/autumn/winter*
le printemps dernier *last spring*
l'été dernier, l'hiver prochain *last summer, next winter*

ce, cette, ces 1. (*this etc* see DEMONSTRATIVES)
  2. **cette nuit, j'ai bien dormi** *I slept well last night;* **ce soir, on ne va pas se coucher tôt** *we won't be going to bed early tonight!*
  3. **ce qui, ce que** (*what, which*): **ce qui m'étonne c'est qu'il ne soit pas parti** *what surprises me is that he hasn't left;* **il a décidé de partir, ce qui nous arrange** *he's decided to go, which is convenient;* **il m'a demandé ce que je faisais** *he asked me what I was doing;* **montre-moi ce qu'il t'a donné** *show me what he gave you*
see also C'EST, QUE, QUESTIONS, QUI, SENTENCES

cela In most cases 'ça' has the same meaning and is in fact more common in speech; when opposed to 'ceci' (*this*), 'cela' means '*that*'

c'est 1. (*it is*) **c'est cher** *it's expensive;* **c'est dommage** *it's* (or: *that's*) *a pity;* **qui c'est?** *who is it?* (*somebody on the phone or at the door*); **c'est la sœur de Gabrielle/le facteur** *it's Gabrielle's sister/the postman*
  2. (*he, she is*) **qui c'est?** *who's he/she?*

(*pointing to somebody*); **who is it?** (*hearing the door bell*); **c'est un journaliste** *he's a journalist;* **c'est une actrice** *she's an actress;* **ce sont mes amis** *they are my friends*

3. **qu'est-ce que c'est? — c'est un ordinateur** *what is it? — it's a computer;* **ce sont des appareils très coûteux** *they are very costly machines*

chacun, chacune
(*each*) **ils ont 10 francs chacun** *they have 10 francs each;* **chacune d'elles doit décider** *each of them must decide;* **si chacun est d'accord** *if everyone agrees*

chaque
1. **chaque page de ce livre** *each page of this book*

2. **ils coûtent 10 francs chaque** *they cost 10 francs each*

3. **nous nous voyons chaque jour** *we see each other every day*

combien
1. **combien de: combien de livres as-tu?** *how many books have you got?;* **combien d'argent as-tu?** *how much money do you have?*

2. **combien de temps: combien de temps resterez-vous?** *how long will you be staying?*

3. (*price, measurement etc*) **combien coûte ce disque?** *how much does this record cost?;* **combien mesurez-vous?** *how tall are you?;* **ça vaut combien?** *how much is it worth?*

comme
1. (*comparison*) **donnez m'en un comme celui-ci** *give me one like this;* **il fait comme tout le monde** *he does the same as everybody*

2. (*time*) **comme je partais, il est entré** *as I was leaving, he came in*

3. (*reason*) **comme il fait froid, je vais prendre le bus** *since it's cold, I'll take the bus*

4. see EXCLAMATIONS

comparative and superlative (for comparisons see also AUSSI, AUTANT)

To form the comparative French places 'plus' (*more*) or 'moins' (*less*) before the adjective or adverb:

un événement **plus récent** *a more recent event*
de **plus belles** histoires *nicer stories*
une rue **moins bruyante** *a less noisy street*
des repas **moins chers** *cheaper meals*

il est **plus grand que** moi *he's taller than me*
je cours **moins vite que** lui *I run less fast than he does*
nous sommes partis **plus tôt qu'**hier *we left earlier than yesterday*

aller **moins vite** *to go more slowly*
partir **plus tôt** *to leave earlier*

To form the superlative, French places 'le/la/les plus' (*the most*) or 'le/la/les moins' (*the least*) before the adjective; and 'le plus/le moins' before the adverb:

le garçon **le plus intelligent** *the most intelligent boy*
l'épicerie **la plus proche** *the nearest grocer's*
les moins beaux... *the least beautiful*...
les robes **les moins chères** *the least expensive dresses*

elle court **le plus/le moins vite** *she runs fastest/slowest*

Points to note:

1. The English equivalent of the French comparative/superlative adjective is often adjective+'-er'/'-est' (*nicer, cheaper, nearest* etc.).

2. The choice of 'le plus', 'la plus' or 'les plus' with an adjective depends on the gender of the noun and on whether it is singular or plural:

   for a masculine singular noun use 'le plus'
   for a feminine singular noun use 'la plus'
   for all plural nouns use 'les plus'

   Note:
   la plus belle fille
   or: la fille **la** plus belle
   c'est mon plus cher souvenir
   or: c'est mon souvenir **le** plus cher

3. c'est le plus grand pays **du** monde *it's the biggest country in the world;* c'est l'église la plus célèbre **de** Paris *it's the most famous church in Paris.* Note that after a superlative French uses **de, du** etc. See also SUBJUNCTIVE

♦ *Irregular Comparatives and Superlatives*
1. *adjectives*

COMPARATIVE	SUPERLATIVE
meilleur *better*	le meilleur *the best*
pire *worse*	le pire *the worst*
moindre *lesser*	le moindre *the least*

2. *adverbs*

ADVERB	COMPARATIVE	SUPERLATIVE
beaucoup *a lot*	plus *more*	le plus *(the) most*
bien *well*	mieux *better*	le mieux *(the) best*
peu *little*	moins *less*	le moins *(the) least*

conjunctions

The use of conjunctions in French is broadly similar to English. However there is one aspect which is different – the use of the SUBJUNCTIVE. Some conjunctions, like 'bien que' or 'pour que' always take the subjunctive. After a verb + 'que' construction, use of the SUBJUNCTIVE depends on whether you are dealing with facts on the one hand or suppositions or wishes on the other

♦ *conjunction + phrase or sentence*
The main 'coordinating conjunctions' are 'mais (*but*), ou (*or*), et (*and*), donc (*therefore*), or (*but, now*), ni (*nor, neither*), car (*because, for*)'
Note the use of 'ni':
je n'ai pas le temps ni l'argent nécessaire
I haven't got the time or the money required
il n'a ni argent ni relations
he has neither money nor connections

♦ *conjunction + subordinate clause*
1. que: je ne savais pas qu'il était parti *I didn't know he had left;* je ne crois pas qu'il viendra *I don't think he'll come;* sais-tu qu'il a plus de trente ans? *did you know he's over thirty?;* je doute qu'il vienne *I doubt whether he'll come;* il faut qu'il vienne *he must come*; note the use of the SUBJUNCTIVE after verbs expressing doubt and wishes
2. *Other conjunctions:*
TIME
quand/lorsque: quand il/lorsqu'il reviendra *when he's back* (note the difference in the use of TENSES)

dès que/aussitôt que: préviens-moi dès qu'il/aussitôt qu'il arrive *let me know as soon as he arrives*
au fur et à mesure que: au fur et à mesure qu'ils arrivaient *as they were coming in*
jusqu'à ce que + SUBJUNCTIVE: continue jusqu'à ce qu'il arrive *go on until he arrives*
pendant que: téléphone-lui pendant que je m'habille *give him a ring while I'm getting dressed*

OBJECTIVE
pour que/afin que + SUBJUNCTIVE: je l'ai fait pour que/afin que nous puissions partir plus tôt *I did it so that we could leave earlier*

CAUSE
parce que: je l'ai aidé parce qu'il était malade *I helped him because he was ill*

CONCESSION
bien que + SUBJUNCTIVE: bien qu'il soit arrivé en retard *although he arrived late*

CONDITION
si: s'il vient *if he comes*
à condition que + SUBJUNCTIVE: à condition qu'il vienne *provided he comes*

See also APRES, AVANT, BIEN, POUR, SANS, TANT

dans 1. (*in*) **il est assis dans le jardin** *he's sitting in the garden*

2. (*into, to*) **je l'ai mis dans le tiroir** *I put it in(to) the drawer;* **il rentre dans son pays** *he's going back home*

3. (*out of, from*) **je l'ai pris dans le tiroir du haut** *I took it out of the top drawer*

4. (*time*) **dans deux mois, ils partent en vacances** *they're going on holiday in two months' time*

de (with 'le': contracted as **du**: with 'les' as **des**)

1. (*belonging to, of*) **le toit de la maison** *the roof of the house;* **à la fin du livre** *at the end of the book;* **la voiture de mes parents** *my parents' car;* **les jouets des enfants** *the children's toys*

2. (*material, size, duration etc specified*) **un mur de pierre** *a stone wall;* **une veste de laine** *a woollen jacket;* **un appartement de 130 m^2** *a flat of 130 square metres;* **un séjour d'une semaine** *a week's stay;* **un enfant de 10 ans** *a 10-year-old child*

DEMONSTRATIVES

3. des années de travail *years of work;* **une foule de gens** *a crowd of people;* **une quantité de livres** *a great number of books*

4. *(from)* **il vient de Paris** *he's coming from Paris; he comes from Paris*

5. *(some, any)* see ARTICLES; see also PREPOSITIONAL CONSTRUCTIONS, VERBAL CONSTRUCTIONS

demonstratives

◆ **ce, cette, cet; ces** — 'this'/'that'; 'these'/'those'
The French equivalent of the demonstrative adjective has the four forms shown above; which one you use depends on whether the noun is masculine or feminine, singular or plural:

SINGULAR	PLURAL
ce + masculine noun	
cette + feminine noun	**ces**
cet + masculine noun beginning with a vowel or h mute	

Thus:

	SINGULAR	PLURAL
MASCULINE	**ce** quartier	**ces** rideaux
	cet objet	**ces** étrangers
	cet hiver	**ces** hôtels
FEMININE	**cette** façon	**ces** fenêtres
	cette année	**ces** excuses
	cette habitude	**ces** haies

ce ... -ci/-là

ce quartier-**ci**	*this district*
ce quartier-**là**	*that district*
cette femme-**ci**	*this woman*
cette femme-**là**	*that woman*
ces fenêtres-**ci**	*these windows*
ces fenêtres-**là**	*those windows*

French adds -ci/-là to the noun, to make the distinction rendered in English by 'this' and 'that'.

◆ **celui, celle, ceux, celles** — 'the one'/'the ones'
quel livre a-t-il choisi? — celui qui coûte 10 francs

which book did he choose? — the one which costs 10 francs
avez-vous vu mes photos: celles que j'ai prises en Espagne?
have you seen my photos — the ones I took in Spain?
quelle jupe préfères-tu: celle de Suzanne ou la mienne?
which skirt do you prefer — Suzanne's or mine?
ses yeux sont moins clairs que ceux de son frère
his eyes are darker than his brother's

A demonstrative pronoun replaces a noun already referred to. In French, the form of the demonstrative pronoun depends on whether the noun referred to is masculine or feminine, singular or plural.

celui	replaces a masculine singular noun
celle	replaces a feminine singular noun
ceux	replaces a masculine plural noun
celles	replaces a feminine plural noun

Points to note:
The demonstrative pronoun is almost always accompanied by one of the following:

a. 'qui' (*who/which*) or 'que' (*which, that*):
   celui qui a le plus d'argent doit payer
   the one who has most money must pay
   prends ceux que tu as achetés
   take the ones you bought

b. 'de' (*of*):
   la beauté de la campagne et celle de la ville
   the beauty of the countryside and that of the town

♦ **celui-ci/-là, celle-ci/-là, ceux-ci/-là, celles-ci/-là**
'this one'/'that one' *etc*

French adds **-ci/-là** to the pronoun to make the distinction rendered in English by 'this one' and 'that one':
lequel voulez-vous: celui-ci ou celui-là?
which one do you want — this one or that one?

In addition, 'celui-ci' *etc* and 'celui-là' *etc* can mean 'the former' and 'the latter' respectively

depuis note the difference in the use of tenses, and the fact that 'depuis' corresponds to 'since' and 'for':

1. (*period of time*) **ils se connaissent depuis deux ans/longtemps** *they have known each other for two years/a long time;* **depuis combien de temps habite-t-il en Ecosse?** *for how long has he been living in Scotland?*

2. (*precise date*) **il pleut depuis le premier septembre/avant-hier** *it's been raining since the first of September/the day before yesterday;* **il pleuvait depuis Noël** *it had been raining since Christmas*

des 1. = 'de' + 'les', see DE

2. (*some, any*) see ARTICLES

desquels, desquelles see SENTENCES

devoir for conjugation, see IRREGULAR VERBS

1. (*obligation*) **devoir faire quelque chose** *to have to do something;* **il a dû tout refaire** *he (has) had to do it all again;* **je dois aller chercher mes billets** *I must go and get my tickets;* **il devrait se dépêcher** *he should hurry up;* **il aurait dû me le dire** *he should have told me*

2. (*likelihood, supposition*) **il doit rentrer ce soir** *he should be coming back tonight;* **il devrait être chez lui** *he should be at home;* **il a dû se tromper de route** *he must have taken the wrong road*

3. (*debt*) **il me doit 10 francs** *he owes me 10 francs*

dont 1. **je vois le toit de sa maison > il habite la maison dont je vois le toit** *I can see the roof of his house > he lives in the house whose roof I can see* **les fenêtres de sa maison sont ouvertes > il habite la maison dont les fenêtres sont ouvertes** *the windows of his house are open > he lives in the house whose windows are open/the house with the open windows*
les clients dont nous connaissons l'adresse *the customers whose address we know*

les gens dont l'adresse est en France *people whose address is in France*

   2. **il est fier de son fils > ce fils dont il est si fier** *he is proud of his son > this son of whom he is so proud* **il est responsable du service du personnel > le service dont il est responsable** *he's in charge of the personnel department > the department he's in charge of*
c'est tout ce dont je me souviens *it's all I remember*
le pays dont il parle *the country he's speaking of*

   3. *(amongst whom or which)* **il y avait plusieurs livres, dont un gros dictionnaire** *there were several books, one of them a big dictionary;* **il y avait quelques étrangers, dont deux Français** *there were several foreigners, two of whom were French*

du 1. = 'de' + 'le', see DE
   2. *(some, any)* see ARTICLES

duquel   see SENTENCES

elle, elles   see PERSONAL PRONOUNS

en 1. *(location: in)* **il habite en France** *he lives in France;* **il passe ses vacances en Suisse** *he spends his holidays in Switzerland*
Note: 'en' is not used with a country or area which is masculine: **il habite au Brésil** *he lives in Brazil*

   2. *(movement: to)* **il va en Angleterre** *he's going to England*
Note: 'en' is not used with a country or area which is masculine: **il va au Mexique** *he's going to Mexico*

   3. *(means of transport)* **en voiture/train** *by car/train*

   4. *(made of)* **un mur en pierre** *a stone wall;* **un plat en verre** *a glass dish*

   5. *(as ...)* **en partant** *as he left;* **il est parti en chantant** *he went away singing*

   6. *(shape or nature)* **en cercle** *in a circle;* **en longueur** *in length;* **en forme de** *in the shape of*

   7. *(state of dress)* **il était en short/en chaussettes** *he was wearing shorts/he was in his socks*

8. (*as a pronoun: of it, of them, some/any*)
j'ai deux livres > j'en ai deux
I have two books > I've two (of them)
il y a trois chaises > il y en a trois
there are three chairs > there are three (of them)
je n'ai pas d'argent/de billets > je n'en ai pas
I don't have any money/tickets > I don't have any
je leur ai donné deux billets > je leur en ai donné deux
I gave them two tickets > I gave them two
as-tu acheté des fruits? > en as-tu acheté?
did you buy fruit? > did you buy any?
combien y a-t-il de chambres? > combien y en a-t-il? *how many bedrooms are there? > how many (of them) are there?*

9. (*corresponds to prepositional construction with 'de'*) **il est fier de son père > il en est fier**
he is proud of his father > he is proud of him
il est responsable du service des réservations > il en est responsable
he's in charge of the bookings department > he's in charge of it
j'ai besoin de ce livre > j'en ai besoin
I need this book > I need it

10. (*as a pronoun*) (*from*) **il vient de l'école > il en vient** *he's coming from school > he's coming from there*
il sortait de chez le coiffeur > il en sortait *he was coming out of the barber's > he was coming out*

11. (*time*) **en avril** *in April;* **en deux heures** *in (the space of) two hours* (compare DANS)

encore 1. (*still*) **il dort encore** *he's still asleep;* **il fait encore du ski** *he still skis*

2. (*again*) **il a encore oublié son dictionnaire** *he's forgotten his dictionary again;* **j'aimerais encore une bière** *I'd like another beer;* **voulez-vous encore de la viande?** *do you want some more meat?;* **j'aimerais le faire encore une fois** *I'd like to do it once more*

3. **pas encore: il n'est pas encore rentré** *he's not*

back yet; **il ne lui a pas encore téléphoné** *he hasn't phoned him yet*

   4. (*to emphasize*) **c'est encore moins cher** *it's even cheaper;* **ils vont encore plus vite** *they go even faster*

est-ce que see QUESTIONS

être as an auxiliary, see VERB FORMS; for conjugation see IRREGULAR VERBS

   1. (*belonging*) see A
   2. (*expressions of time*) see TIME

eux see PERSONAL PRONOUNS

exclamations & interjections

WARNINGS, INSTRUCTIONS
attention! *look out!*
dépêchez-vous! *hurry up!*
taisez-vous! *be quiet!*
allez-vous-en! *go away!*
tiens!, tenez! *here you are (handing something)*
ça suffit! *that's enough!*

PROBLEMS
au secours! *help!*
au feu! *fire!*
au voleur! *stop thief!*
qu'est-ce qu'il y a?, qu'y a-t-il?
what's the matter?, what's wrong?
qu'est-ce que vous avez?
what's wrong with you?

EMPHASIS, DEGREE etc
quel dommage! *what a pity!*
quelle surprise! *what a surprise!*
comme elle a grandi! *how she's grown!*
comme elle est jolie! *isn't she pretty!*
qu'il fait chaud! *it's so hot!*

AGREEMENT
d'accord! *O.K.*
je vous en prie *please do*

SURPRISE
tiens! *well, well!*
ah oui? *really?*

GREETINGS

On meeting a stranger

bonjour (Monsieur) *hello;*
 (*plural* Messieurs) *good morning;*
 (Madame) *good afternoon*
 (*plural* Mesdames)
 (Mademoiselle)
 (*plural* Mesdemoiselles)

also: bonsoir (etc) *good evening; good night*

On meeting a friend
bonjour *hello*
salut! *hi!*
ça va? *how are things?*

On leaving a stranger
au revoir (Monsieur) *goodbye*
 (Madame)
 (Mademoiselle)

On leaving a friend
au revoir *goodbye*
salut! *cheerio!*
à tout à l'heure! *see you later!*

Other greetings

bon anniversaire! *happy birthday!*
bonne chance! *good luck!*
bon appétit! *enjoy your meal!*
félicitations! *congratulations!*
joyeux Noël! *Happy Christmas!*
bonne année! *Happy New Year!*
joyeuses Pâques! *Happy Easter!*

faire for conjugation see IRREGULAR VERBS

1. (*sports*) **il fait du ski** *he skis, he goes skiing;* **dimanche il est allé faire de la voile/du tennis** *on Sunday he went sailing/played tennis*

2. **qu'est-ce que vous faites?** (*as a job*) *what do you do?;* (*just now*) *what are you doing?*

3. (*with prices or measurements*) **ça fait 10 francs** *it's 10 francs;* **ça fait 10 kilomètres** *it's 10 kilometres*

FALLOIR

4. (*weather*) **il fait froid/chaud** *it's cold/warm*

5. (*time: ago, since*) **ça fait trois semaines que je l'attends** *I've been waiting for him for three weeks now;* **ça fait trois ans qu'il s'est marié** *it's three years since he got married, he got married three years ago;* note the difference in the use of TENSES; see also DEPUIS, IL Y A

6. ne faire que...: il ne fait que se plaindre *he complains all the time, he does nothing but complain;* **il n'a fait que son devoir** *he was only doing his duty*

7. (*in combination with another verb: cause to do or be done*) **faire réparer quelque chose** *to get something repaired;* **il a fait tomber la bouteille** *he knocked the bottle over;* **faire travailler ses employés** *to make one's employees work;* **faire partir la voiture** *to get the car to start*

falloir for conjugation see IRREGULAR VERBS

1. (*requirement*) **il faut trois heures pour aller à...** *it takes three hours to go to...;* **il faut quatre œufs pour une omelette** *you need four eggs for an omelette, four eggs are needed for an omelette*

2. (*obligation*) **il a fallu partir** *we had to leave;* **il faudra penser à écrire** *I'll (you'll etc) have to think about writing;* **il faut dire que...** *it must be said that...;* **il ne faut pas y toucher** *you mustn't touch it, you've not to touch it*

3. il faut que...: il faut que son père lui écrive *his father will have to write to him, his father must write to him;* note the use of the SUBJUNCTIVE

feminine see GENDER

gender
In French, all nouns are either masculine or feminine. Don't assume, however, that masculine always equals 'male' and feminine 'female'. Certain nouns are masculine or feminine according to meaning — 'l'homme' (the man), 'le garçon' (the boy) are masculine; 'la femme' (the woman), 'la fille' (the girl) are feminine —, but most others, such as 'le livre' (the book) or 'la chaise' (the chair) cannot be described as being male or female

GENDER

A word which is only masculine or only feminine in French may have an English equivalent which can be either male or female:

la sentinelle *(male/female) guard*
le témoin *(male/female) witness*
la victime *(male/female) victim*

By and large, therefore, you cannot predict gender: you must learn it along with the noun. And in the case of certain nouns whose meanings vary according to gender, you run the risk of completely changing the sense of what you want to say if you get the gender wrong. Listed below are the most common of those nouns:

MASCULINE		FEMININE	
le livre	*book*	**la** livre	*pound*
le manche	*handle*	**la** manche	*sleeve*
le mémoire	*memo*	**la** mémoire	*memory*
le page	*page boy*	**la** page	*page (of book)*
le poêle	*stove*	**la** poêle	*frying pan*
le poste	*post, job*	**la** poste	*post, mail*
le tour	*turn*	**la** tour	*tower*
le somme	*nap*	**la** somme	*sum*
le vapeur	*steamer*	**la** vapeur	*steam*
le voile	*veil*	**la** voile	*sail*

◆ *Feminine equivalents of masculine nouns*

Male and female pairs may have distinctly separate forms: 'le frère' (the brother); 'la sœur' (the sister); 'le mari' (the husband); 'la femme' (the wife)

Usually however, the feminine differs from the masculine in these cases by a feminine ending, ie. 'acteur/actrice' (actor/actress); 'hôte/hôtesse' (host/hostess); 'lion/lionne' (lion/lioness)

The most common of these endings is '-e' which is added to the masculine singular noun unless it already ends in an '–e' (see PRONUNCIATION):

MASCULINE	FEMININE
le cousin	la cousine
l'ami	l'amie
le camarade	la camarade

Other endings are:

MASCULINE	FEMININE
le veuf	la veuve
l'époux	l'épouse
le jumeau	la jumelle
l'Italien	l'Italienne
le paysan	la paysanne
le lion	la lionne
le berger	la bergère
l'infirmier	l'infirmière
le danseur	la danseuse
l'acteur	l'actrice
l'hôte	l'hôtesse

greetings see EXCLAMATIONS

il, ils see PERSONAL PRONOUNS.

il y a 1. (*there is/are*) **il y a un livre/des livres sur la table** *there is a book/are some books on the table;* **il y a trop de monde** *there are too many people;* **il n'y avait personne** *there wasn't anybody there;* **il n'y a pas de train le matin** *there's no train in the morning;* **y aura-t-il beaucoup de monde?** *will there be many people?;* **y a-t-il assez de sucre?** *is there enough sugar?*

2. (*time*) **il y a deux ans que je suis parti** *I left two years ago, it's two years since I left;* **il n'y a pas longtemps que je le connais** *I haven't known him for very long;* **il y a combien de temps que vous habitez à Paris?** *how long have you been living in Paris?* see also DEPUIS, FAIRE

3. **il n'y a qu'à nous le dire** *you only need to say, just tell us*

4. **qu'est-ce qu'il y a?** *what's the matter?*

imperatives e.g. **taisez-vous!** *be quiet!*

For regular verbs use the 'tu'*, 'nous' and 'vous' forms of the present tense minus their subject pronouns:

DONNER	FINIR	VENDRE
donne*	finis	vends
donnons	finissons	vendons
donnez	finissez	vendez

* for '-er' verbs (and some '-ir' verbs e.g. 'couvrir', 'ouvrir') the 's' of the present tense is dropped in the imperative, except when followed by Y or EN e.g. 'vas-y'; 'plantes-en'.

donne son livre au garçon — *give the boy his book*
finissons notre travail — *let's finish our work*
vendez la maison — *sell the house*

Note:

1. In **positive commands** object pronouns **follow** the verb and are joined to it by a hyphen:

    donne-**le-lui** — *give it to him*
    finissons-**le** — *let's finish it*
    vendez-**la** — *sell it*

2. In **negative commands** object pronouns **come before** the verb, and are not attached to it:

    ne **le lui** donne pas — *don't give it to him*
    ne **le** finissons pas — *let's not finish it*
    ne **la** vendez pas — *don't sell it*

3. For REFLEXIVE VERBS the appropriate form of the reflexive pronoun must go with the verb in the imperative:

    assieds-**toi** — *sit down*
    levez-**vous** — *stand up*
    arrêtons-**nous** ici — *let's stop here*

    ne **t'**assieds pas — *don't sit down*
    ne **vous** levez pas — *don't stand up*
    ne **nous** arrêtons pas ici — *let's not stop here*

4. The imperative forms of 'avoir' and 'être' are irregular:

AVOIR	ÊTRE
aie	sois
ayons	soyons
ayez	soyez

    e.g. n'**ayez** pas peur *don't be afraid*
    sois sage *be good*

interjections see EXCLAMATIONS

IRREGULAR VERBS

irregular verbs The conjugation of regular verbs is explained at the entry VERB FORMS, where three models are shown ('donner' for '-er' verbs, 'finir' for '-ir' verbs, and 'vendre' for '-re' verbs). The main irregular verbs are listed below, with forms for all main tenses (for compound tenses see VERB FORMS)

abattre (*to pull down*) conjugation *see* **battre**

aboyer (*to bark*) conjugation like 'donner' (i.e. regular), but in some tenses subject to predictable spelling changes: see VERB FORMS

abréger (*to shorten*) conjugation like 'donner' (i.e. regular), but in some tenses subject to predictable spelling changes: see VERB FORMS

absoudre (*to absolve*) conjugation *see* **résoudre**, except for the following:
 4. *PAST HISTORIC not in current use*
 7. *PAST PARTICIPLE* absous

accélérer (*to accelerate*) conjugation like 'donner' (i.e. regular), but in some tenses subject to predictable spelling changes: see VERB FORMS

accueillir (*to welcome*) conjugation *see* **cueillir**

acheter (*to buy*) conjugation like 'donner' (i.e. regular), but in some tenses subject to predictable spelling changes: see VERB FORMS

acquérir (*to acquire*) auxiliary 'avoir': j'ai acquis
 1. *PRESENT* j'acquiers, tu acquiers, il/elle acquiert, nous acquérons, vous acquérez, ils/elles acquièrent
 2. *PRESENT SUBJUNCTIVE* j'acquière, tu acquières, il/elle acquière, nous acquérions, vous acquériez, ils/elles acquièrent
 3. *IMPERFECT* j'acquérais, tu acquérais, il/elle acquérait, nous acquérions, vous acquériez, ils/elles acquéraient
 4. *PAST HISTORIC* j'acquis, tu acquis, il/elle acquit, nous acquîmes, vous acquîtes, ils/elles acquirent
 5. *FUTURE* j'acquerrai. tu acquerras, il/elle acquerra, nous acquerrons, vous acquerrez, ils/elles acquerront

6. *CONDITIONAL* j'acquerrais, tu acquerrais, il/elle acquerrait, nous acquerrions, vous acquerriez, ils/elles acquerraient

7. *PAST PARTICIPLE* acquis

8. *PRESENT PARTICIPLE* acquérant

admettre (*to admit*) conjugation see **mettre**

advenir (*to happen*) auxiliary 'être': il est advenu *etc;* impersonal, 3rd person only

1. *PRESENT* il advient
2. *PRESENT SUBJUNCTIVE* il advienne
3. *IMPERFECT* il advenait
4. *PAST HISTORIC* il advint
5. *FUTURE* il adviendra
6. *CONDITIONAL* il adviendrait
7. *PAST PARTICIPLE* advenu
8. *PRESENT PARTICIPLE* advenant

agacer (*to annoy*) conjugation like 'donner' (i.e. regular), but in some tenses subject to predictable spelling changes: see VERB FORMS

aller (*to go*) auxiliary 'être': je suis allé *etc*

1. *PRESENT* je vais, tu vas, il/elle va, nous allons, vous allez, ils/elles vont
2. *PRESENT SUBJUNCTIVE* j'aille, tu ailles, il/elle aille, nous allions, vous alliez, ils/elles aillent
3. *IMPERFECT* j'allais, tu allais, il/elle allait, nous allions, vous alliez, ils/elles allaient
4. *PAST HISTORIC* j'allai, tu allas, il/elle alla, nous allâmes, vous allâtes, ils/elles allèrent
5. *FUTURE* j'irai, tu iras, il/elle ira, nous irons, vous irez, ils/elles iront
6. *CONDITIONAL* j'irais, tu irais, il/elle irait, nous irions, vous iriez, ils/elles iraient
7. *PAST PARTICIPLE* allé
8. *PRESENT PARTICIPLE* allant

amener (*to bring*) conjugation like 'donner' (i.e. regular), but in some tenses subject to predictable spelling changes: see VERB FORMS

annoncer (*to announce*) conjugation like 'donner' (i.e. regular), but in some tenses subject to

36 IRREGULAR VERBS

predictable spelling changes: see VERB FORMS

apercevoir (*to see*) conjugation *see* **recevoir**

apparaître (*to appear*) conjugation *see* **paraître**

appartenir (*to belong*) conjugation *see* **tenir**

appeler (*to call*) conjugation like 'donner' (i.e. regular), but in some tenses subject to predictable spelling changes: see VERB FORMS

apprendre (*to learn*) conjugation *see* **prendre**

appuyer (*to push*) conjugation like 'donner' (i.e. regular), but in some tenses subject to predictable spelling changes: see VERB FORMS

arranger (*to arrange*) conjugation like 'donner' (i.e. regular), but in some tenses subject to predictable spelling changes: see VERB FORMS

assaillir (*to assault*) auxiliary 'avoir': j'ai assailli *etc*

1. *PRESENT* j'assaille, tu assailles, il/elle assaille, nous assaillons, vous assaillez, ils/elles assaillent

2. *PRESENT SUBJUNCTIVE* j'assaille, tu assailles, il/elle assaille, nous assaillions, vous assailliez, ils/elles assaillent

3. *IMPERFECT* j'assaillais, tu assaillais, il/elle assaillait, nous assaillions, vous assailliez, ils/elles assaillaient

4. *PAST HISTORIC* j'assaillis, tu assaillis, il/elle assaillit, nous assaillîmes, vous assaillîtes, ils/elles assaillirent

5. *FUTURE* j'assaillirai, tu assailliras, il/elle assaillira, nous assaillirons, vous assaillirez, ils/elles assailliront

6. *CONDITIONAL* j'assaillirais, tu assaillirais, il/elle assaillirait, nous assaillirions, vous assailliriez, ils/elles assailliraient

7. *PAST PARTICIPLE* assailli

8. *PRESENT PARTICIPLE* assaillant

s'asseoir (*to sit down*) auxiliary 'être': je me suis assis *etc*

1. *PRESENT* je m'assieds, tu t'assieds, il/elle

IRREGULAR VERBS

s'assied, nous nous asseyons, vous vous asseyez, ils/elles s'asseyent

2. *PRESENT SUBJUNCTIVE* je m'asseye, tu t'asseyes, il/elle s'asseye, nous nous asseyions, vous vous asseyiez, ils/elles s'asseyent

3. *IMPERFECT* je m'asseyais, tu t'asseyais, il/elle s'asseyait, nous nous asseyions, vous vous asseyiez, ils/elles s'asseyaient

4. *PAST HISTORIC* je m'assis, tu t'assis, il/elle s'assit, nous nous assîmes, vous vous assîtes, ils/elles s'assirent

5. *FUTURE* je m'assiérai, tu t'assiéras, il/elle s'assiéra, nous nous assiérons, vous vous assiérez, ils/elles s'assiéront

6. *CONDITIONAL* je m'assiérais, tu t'assiérais, il/elle s'assiérait, nous nous assiérions, vous vous assiériez, ils/elles s'assiéraient

7. *PAST PARTICIPLE* assis

8. *PRESENT PARTICIPLE* s'asseyant

atteindre (*to reach*) conjugation *see* **teindre**

avancer (*to advance*) conjugation like 'donner' (i.e. regular), but in some tenses subject to predictable spelling changes: see VERB FORMS

avoir (*to have*) auxiliary 'avoir': j'ai eu *etc*

1. *PRESENT* j'ai, tu as, il/elle a, nous avons, vous avez, ils/elles ont

2. *PRESENT SUBJUNCTIVE* j'aie, tu aies, il/elle ait, nous ayons, vous ayez, ils/elles aient

3. *IMPERFECT* j'avais, tu avais, il/elle avait, nous avions, vous aviez, ils/elles avaient

4. *PAST HISTORIC* j'eus, tu eus, il/elle eut, nous eûmes, vous eûtes, ils/elles eurent

5. *FUTURE* j'aurai, tu auras, il/elle aura, nous aurons, vous aurez, ils/elles auront

6. *CONDITIONAL* j'aurais, tu aurais, il/elle aurait, nous aurions, vous auriez, ils/elles auraient

7. *PAST PARTICIPLE* eu

8. *PRESENT PARTICIPLE* ayant

38 IRREGULAR VERBS

balayer (*to sweep*) conjugation like 'donner' (i.e. regular), but in some tenses subject to predictable spelling changes: see VERB FORMS

battre (*to beat*) auxiliary 'avoir': j'ai battu *etc*
1. *PRESENT* je bats, tu bats, il/elle bat, nous battons, vous battez, ils/elles battent
2. *PRESENT SUBJUNCTIVE* je batte, tu battes, il/elle batte, nous battions, vous battiez, ils/elles battent
3. *IMPERFECT* je battais, tu battais, il/elle battait, nous battions, vous battiez, ils/elles battaient
4. *PAST HISTORIC* je battis, tu battis, il/elle battit, nous battîmes, vous battîtes, ils/elles battirent
5. *FUTURE* je battrai, tu battras, il/elle battra, nous battrons, vous battrez, ils/elles battront
6. *CONDITIONAL* je battrais, tu battrais, il/elle battrait, nous battrions, vous battriez, ils/elles battraient
7. *PAST PARTICIPLE* battu
8. *PRESENT PARTICIPLE* battant

bercer (*to rock*) conjugation like 'donner' (i.e. regular), but in some tenses subject to predictable spelling changes: see VERB FORMS

boire (*to drink*) auxiliary 'avoir': j'ai bu *etc*
1. *PRESENT* je bois, tu bois, il/elle boit, nous buvons, vous buvez, ils/elles boivent
2. *PRESENT SUBJUNCTIVE* je boive, tu boives, il/elle boive, nous buvions, vous buviez, ils/elles boivent
3. *IMPERFECT* je buvais, tu buvais, il/elle buvait, nous buvions, vous buviez, ils/elles buvaient
4. *PAST HISTORIC* je bus, tu bus, il/elle but, nous bûmes, vous bûtes, ils/elles burent
5. *FUTURE* je boirai, tu boiras, il/elle boira, nous boirons, vous boirez, ils/elles boiront
6. *CONDITIONAL* je boirais, tu boirais, il/elle boirait, nous boirions, vous boiriez, ils/elles boiraient
7. *PAST PARTICIPLE* bu
8. *PRESENT PARTICIPLE* buvant

bouger (*to move*) conjugation like 'donner' (i.e. regular), but in some tenses subject to predictable

IRREGULAR VERBS

spelling changes: see VERB FORMS

bouillir (*to boil*) auxiliary 'avoir': j'ai bouilli *etc*
1. *PRESENT* je bous, tu bous, il/elle bout, nous bouillons, vous bouillez, ils/elles bouillent
2. *PRESENT SUBJUNCTIVE* je bouille, tu bouilles, il/elle bouille, nous bouillions, vous bouilliez, ils/elles bouillent
3. *IMPERFECT* je bouillais, tu bouillais, il/elle bouillait, nous bouillions, vous bouilliez, ils/elles bouillaient
4. *PAST HISTORIC* je bouillis, tu bouillis, il/elle bouillit, nous bouillîmes, vous bouillîtes, ils/elles bouillirent
5. *FUTURE* je bouillirai, tu bouilliras, il/elle bouillira, nous bouillirons, vous bouillirez, ils/elles bouilliront
6. *CONDITIONAL* je bouillirais, tu bouillirais, il/elle bouillirait, nous bouillirions, vous bouilliriez, ils/elles bouilliraient
7. *PAST PARTICIPLE* bouilli
8. *PRESENT PARTICIPLE* bouillant

céder (*to give up*) conjugation like 'donner' (i.e. regular), but in some tenses subject to predictable spelling changes: see VERB FORMS

célébrer (*to celebrate*) conjugation like 'donner' (i.e. regular), but in some tenses subject to predictable spelling changes: see VERB FORMS

changer (*to change*) conjugation like 'donner' (i.e. regular), but in some tenses subject to predictable spelling changes: see VERB FORMS

charger (*to load*) conjugation like 'donner' (i.e. regular), but in some tenses subject to predictable spelling changes: see VERB FORMS

commencer (*to begin*) conjugation like 'donner' (i.e. regular), but in some tenses subject to predictable spelling changes: see VERB FORMS

commettre (*to commit*) conjugation *see* **mettre**

compléter (*to complete*) conjugation like 'donner'

40 IRREGULAR VERBS

(i.e. regular), but in some tenses subject to predictable spelling changes: see VERB FORMS

comprendre (*to understand*) conjugation *see* **prendre**

conclure (*to conclude*) auxiliary 'avoir': j'ai conclu *etc*

1. *PRESENT* je conclus, tu conclus, il/elle conclut, nous concluons, vous concluez, ils/elles concluent
2. *PRESENT SUBJUNCTIVE* je conclue, tu conclues, il/elle conclue, nous concluions, vous concluiez, ils/elles concluent
3. *IMPERFECT* je concluais, tu concluais, il/elle concluait, nous concluions, vous concluiez, ils/elles concluaient
4. *PAST HISTORIC* je conclus, tu conclus, il/elle conclut, nous conclûmes, vous conclûtes, ils/elles conclurent
5. *FUTURE* je conclurai, tu concluras, il/elle conclura, nous conclurons, vous conclurez, ils/elles concluront
6. *CONDITIONAL* je conclurais, tu conclurais, il/elle conclurait, nous conclurions, vous concluriez, ils/elles concluraient
7. *PAST PARTICIPLE* conclu
8. *PRESENT PARTICIPLE* concluant

conduire (*to drive*) conjugation *see* **cuire**

connaître (*to know*) auxiliary 'avoir': j'ai connu *etc*

1. *PRESENT* je connais, tu connais, il/elle connaît, nous connaissons, vous connaissez, ils/elles connaissent
2. *PRESENT SUBJUNCTIVE* je connaisse, tu connaisses, il/elle connaisse, nous connaissions, vous connaissiez, ils/elles connaissent
3. *IMPERFECT* je connaissais, tu connaissais, il/elle connaissait, nous connaissions, vous connaissiez, ils/elles connaissaient
4. *PAST HISTORIC* je connus, tu connus, il/elle connut, nous connûmes, vous connûtes, ils/elles connurent
5. *FUTURE* je connaîtrai, tu connaîtras, il/elle

connaîtra, nous connaîtrons, vous connaîtrez, ils/elles connaîtront

6. *CONDITIONAL* je connaîtrais, tu connaîtrais, il/elle connaîtrait, nous connaîtrions, vous connaîtriez, ils/elles connaîtraient

7. *PAST PARTICIPLE* connu

8. *PRESENT PARTICIPLE* connaissant

consentir (*to agree*) conjugation *see* **sentir**

construire (*to build*) conjugation *see* **cuire**

convaincre (*to convince*) conjugation *see* **vaincre**

convenir (*to agree*) conjugation *see* **venir**, but auxiliary 'avoir': j'ai convenu *etc*

coudre (*to sew*) auxiliary 'avoir': j'ai cousu *etc*

1. *PRESENT* je couds, tu couds, il/elle coud, nous cousons, vous cousez, ils/elles cousent

2. *PRESENT SUBJUNCTIVE* je couse, tu couses, il/elle couse, nous cousions, vous cousiez, ils/elles cousent

3. *IMPERFECT* je cousais, tu cousais, il/elle cousait, nous cousions, vous cousiez, ils/elles cousaient

4. *PAST HISTORIC* je cousis, tu cousis, il/elle cousit, nous cousîmes, vous cousîtes, ils/elles cousirent

5. *FUTURE* je coudrai, tu coudras, il/elle coudra, nous coudrons, vous coudrez, ils/elles coudront

6. *CONDITIONAL* je coudrais, tu coudrais, il/elle coudrait, nous coudrions, vous coudriez, ils/elles coudraient

7. *PAST PARTICIPLE* cousu

8. *PRESENT PARTICIPLE* cousant

courir (*to run*) auxiliary 'avoir': j'ai couru *etc*

1. *PRESENT* je cours, tu cours, il/elle court, nous courons, vous courez, ils/elles courent

2. *PRESENT SUBJUNCTIVE* je coure, tu coures, il/elle coure, nous courions, vous couriez, ils/elles courent

3. *IMPERFECT* je courais, tu courais, il/elle courait, nous courions, vous couriez, ils/elles couraient

4. *PAST HISTORIC* je courus, tu courus, il/elle courut, nous courûmes, vous courûtes, ils/elles coururent

5. *FUTURE* je courrai, tu courras, il/elle courra, nous courrons, vous courrez, ils/elles courront

42 IRREGULAR VERBS

6. *CONDITIONAL* je courrais, tu courrais, il/elle courrait, nous courrions, vous courriez, ils/elles courraient

7. *PAST PARTICIPLE* couru

8. *PRESENT PARTICIPLE* courant

couvrir (*to cover*) auxiliary 'avoir': j'ai couvert *etc*

1. *PRESENT* je couvre, tu couvres, il/elle couvre, nous couvrons, vous couvrez, ils/elles couvrent

2. *PRESENT SUBJUNCTIVE* je couvre, tu couvres, il/elle couvre, nous couvrions, vous couvriez, ils/elles couvrent

3. *IMPERFECT* je couvrais, tu couvrais, il/elle couvrait, nous couvrions, vous couvriez, ils/elles couvraient

4. *PAST HISTORIC* je couvris, tu couvris, il/elle couvrit, nous couvrîmes, vous couvrîtes, ils/elles couvrirent

5. *FUTURE* je couvrirai, tu couvriras, il/elle couvrira, nous couvrirons, vous couvrirez, ils/elles couvriront

6. *CONDITIONAL* je couvrirais, tu couvrirais, il/elle couvrirait, nous couvririons, vous couvririez, ils/elles couvriraient

7. *PAST PARTICIPLE* couvert

8. *PRESENT PARTICIPLE* couvrant

craindre (*to fear*) auxiliary 'avoir': j'ai craint *etc*

1. *PRESENT* je crains, tu crains, il/elle craint, nous craignons, vous craignez, ils/elles craignent

2. *PRESENT SUBJUNCTIVE* je craigne, tu craignes, il/elle craigne, nous craignions, vous craigniez, ils/elles craignent

3. *IMPERFECT* je craignais, tu craignais, il/elle craignait, nous craignions, vous craigniez, ils/elles craignaient

4. *PAST HISTORIC* je craignis, tu craignis, il/elle craignit, nous craignîmes, vous craignîtes, ils/elles craignirent

5. *FUTURE* je craindrai, tu craindras, il/elle craindra, nous craindrons, vous craindrez, ils/elles craindront

IRREGULAR VERBS

6. *CONDITIONAL* je craindrais, tu craindras, il/elle craindrait, nous craindrions, vous craindriez, ils/elles craindraient
7. *PAST PARTICIPLE* craint
8. *PRESENT PARTICIPLE* craignant

crier (*to shout*) conjugation is regular, but note the following:
2. *PRESENT SUBJUNCTIVE* je crie, tu cries, il/elle crie, nous criions, vous criiez, ils/elles crient
3. *IMPERFECT* je criais, tu criais, il/elle criait, nous criions, vous criiez, ils/elles criaient
5. *FUTURE* je crierai *etc*

croire (*to believe*) auxiliary 'avoir': j'ai cru *etc*
1. *PRESENT* je crois, tu crois, il/elle croit, nous croyons, vous croyez, ils/elles croient
2. *PRESENT SUBJUNCTIVE* je croie, tu croies, il/elle croie, nous croyions, vous croyiez, ils/elles croient
3. *IMPERFECT* je croyais, tu croyais, il/elle croyait, nous croyions, vous croyiez, ils/elles croyaient
4. *PAST HISTORIC* je crus, tu crus, il/elle crut, nous crûmes, vous crûtes, ils/elles crurent
5. *FUTURE* je croirai, tu croiras, il/elle croira, nous croirons, vous croirez, ils/elles croiront
6. *CONDITIONAL* je croirais, tu croirais, il/elle croirait, nous croirions, vous croiriez, ils/elles croiraient
7. *PAST PARTICIPLE* cru
8. *PRESENT PARTICIPLE* croyant

croître (*to grow*) auxiliary 'avoir': j'ai crû *etc*
1. *PRESENT* je croîs, tu croîs, il/elle croît, nous croissons, vous croissez, ils/elles croissent
2. *PRESENT SUBJUNCTIVE* je croisse, tu croisses, il/elle croisse, nous croissions, vous croissiez, ils/elles croissent
3. *IMPERFECT* je croissais, tu croissais, il/elle croissait, nous croissions, vous croissiez, ils/elles croissaient
4. *PAST HISTORIC* je crûs, tu crûs, il/elle crût, nous crûmes, vous crûtes, ils/elles crûrent

44 IRREGULAR VERBS

5. *FUTURE* je croîtrai, tu croîtras, il/elle croîtra, nous croîtrons, vous croîtrez, ils/elles croîtront

6. *CONDITIONAL* je croîtrais, tu croîtrais, il/elle croîtrait, nous croîtrions, vous croîtriez, ils/elles croîtraient

7. *PAST PARTICIPLE* crû

8. *PRESENT PARTICIPLE* croissant

cueillir (*to pick*) auxiliary 'avoir': j'ai cueilli *etc*

1. *PRESENT* je cueille, tu cueilles, il/elle cueille, nous cueillons, vous cueillez, ils/elles cueillent

2. *PRESENT SUBJUNCTIVE* je cueille, tu cueilles, il/elle cueille, nous cueillions, vous cueilliez, ils/elles cueillent

3. *IMPERFECT* je cueillais, tu cueillais, il/elle cueillait, nous cueillions, vous cueilliez, ils/elles cueillaient

4. *PAST HISTORIC* je cueillis, tu cueillis, il/elle cueillit, nous cueillîmes, vous cueillîtes, ils/elles cueillirent

5. *FUTURE* je cueillerai, tu cueilleras, il/elle cueillera, nous cueillerons, vous cueillerez, ils/elles cueilleront

6. *CONDITIONAL* je cueillerais, tu cueillerais, il/elle cueillerait, nous cueillerions, vous cueilleriez, ils/elles cueilleraient

7. *PAST PARTICIPLE* cueilli

8. *PRESENT PARTICIPLE* cueillant

cuire (*to cook*) auxiliary 'avoir': j'ai cuit *etc*

1. *PRESENT* je cuis, tu cuis, il/elle cuit, nous cuisons, vous cuisez, ils/elles cuisent

2. *PRESENT SUBJUNCTIVE* je cuise, tu cuises, il/elle cuise, nous cuisions, vous cuisiez, ils/elles cuisent

3. *IMPERFECT* je cuisais, tu cuisais, il/elle cuisait, nous cuisions, vous cuisiez, ils/elles cuisaient

4. *PAST HISTORIC* je cuisis, tu cuisis, il/elle cuisit, nous cuisîmes, vous cuisîtes, ils/elles cuisirent

5. *FUTURE* je cuirai, tu cuiras, il/elle cuira, nous cuirons, vous cuirez, ils/elles cuiront

6. *CONDITIONAL* je cuirais, tu cuirais, il/elle cuirait, nous cuirions, vous cuiriez, ils/elles cuiraient

7. *PAST PARTICIPLE* cuit
8. *PRESENT PARTICIPLE* cuisant

décevoir (*to disappoint*) conjugation *see* **recevoir**

décourager (*to discourage*) conjugation like 'donner' (i.e. regular), but in some tenses subject to predictable spelling changes. see VERB FORMS

découvrir (*to discover*) conjugation *see* **couvrir**

décrire (*to describe*) conjugation *see* **écrire**

décroître (*to diminish*) auxiliary 'avoir': j'ai décru *etc*

1. *PRESENT* je décrois, tu décrois, il/elle décroit, nous décroissons, vous décroissez, ils/elles décroissent
2. *PRESENT SUBJUNCTIVE* je décroisse, tu décroisses, il/elle décroisse, nous décroissions, vous décroissiez, ils/elles décroissent
3. *IMPERFECT* je décroissais, tu décroissais, il/elle décroissait, nous décroissions, vous décroissiez, ils/elles décroissaient
4. *PAST HISTORIC* je décrus, tu décrus, il/elle décrut, nous décrûmes, vous décrûtes, ils/elles décrurent
5. *FUTURE* je décroîtrai, tu décroîtras, il/elle décroîtra, nous décroîtrons, vous décroîtrez, ils/elles décroîtront
6. *CONDITIONAL* je décroîtrais, tu décroîtrais, il/elle décroîtrait, nous décroîtrions, vous décroîtriez, ils/elles décroîtraient
7. *PAST PARTICIPLE* décru
8. *PRESENT PARTICIPLE* décroissant

dégager (*to free*) conjugation like 'donner' (i.e. regular), but in some tenses subject to predictable spelling changes: see VERB FORMS

déménager (*to move*) conjugation like 'donner' (i.e. regular), but in some tenses subject to predictable spelling changes: see VERB FORMS

détruire (*to destroy*) conjugation *see* **cuire**

devenir (*to become*) conjugation *see* **venir**

devoir (*to have to, owe*) auxiliary 'avoir': j'ai dû *etc*

IRREGULAR VERBS

1. *PRESENT* je dois, tu dois, il/elle doit, nous devons, vous devez, ils/elles doivent
2. *PRESENT SUBJUNCTIVE* je doive, tu doives, il/elle doive, nous devions, vous deviez, ils/elles doivent
3. *IMPERFECT* je devais, tu devais, il/elle devait, nous devions, vous deviez, ils/elles devaient
4. *PAST HISTORIC* je dus, tu dus, il/elle dut, nous dûmes, vous dûtes, ils/elles durent
5. *FUTURE* je devrai, tu devras, il/elle devra, nous devrons, vous devrez, ils/elles devront
6. *CONDITIONAL* je devrais, tu devrais, il/elle devrait, nous devrions, vous devriez, ils/elles devraient
7. *PAST PARTICIPLE* dû
8. *PRESENT PARTICIPLE* devant

dire (*to say*) auxiliary 'avoir': j'ai dit *etc*
1. *PRESENT* je dis, tu dis, il/elle dit, nous disons, vous dites, ils/elles disent
2. *PRESENT SUBJUNCTIVE* je dise, tu dises, il/elle dise, nous disions, vous disiez, ils/elles disent
3. *IMPERFECT* je disais, tu disais, il/elle disait, nous disions, vous disiez, ils/elles disaient
4. *PAST HISTORIC* je dis, tu dis, il/elle dit, nous dîmes, vous dîtes, ils/elles dirent
5. *FUTURE* je dirai, tu diras, il/elle dira, nous dirons, vous direz, ils/elles diront
6. *CONDITIONAL* je dirais, tu dirais, il/elle dirait, nous dirions, vous diriez, ils/elles diraient
7. *PAST PARTICIPLE* dit
8. *PRESENT PARTICIPLE* disant

diriger (*to direct*) conjugation like 'donner' (i.e. regular), but in some tenses subject to predictable spelling changes: see VERB FORMS

disparaître (*to disappear*) conjugation *see* paraître

dormir (*to sleep*) auxiliary 'avoir': j'ai dormi *etc*
1. *PRESENT* je dors, tu dors, il/elle dort, nous dormons, vous dormez, ils/elles dorment
2. *PRESENT SUBJUNCTIVE* je dorme, tu dormes,

il/elle dorme, nous dormions, vous dormiez, ils/elles dorment

3. *IMPERFECT* je dormais, tu dormais, il/elle dormait, nous dormions, vous dormiez, ils/elles dormaient

4. *PAST HISTORIC* je dormis, tu dormis, il/elle dormit, nous dormîmes, vous dormîtes, ils/elles dormirent

5. *FUTURE* je dormirai, tu dormiras, il/elle dormira, nous dormirons, vous dormirez, ils/elles dormiront

6. *CONDITIONAL* je dormirais, tu dormirais, il/elle dormirait, nous dormirions, vous dormiriez, ils/elles dormiraient

7. *PAST PARTICIPLE* dormi

8. *PRESENT PARTICIPLE* dormant

écrire (*to write*) auxiliary 'avoir': j'ai écrit *etc*

1. *PRESENT* j'écris, tu écris, il/elle écrit, nous écrivons, vous écrivez, ils/elles écrivent

2. *PRESENT SUBJUNCTIVE* j'écrive, tu écrives, il/elle écrive, nous écrivions, vous écriviez, ils/elles écrivent

3. *IMPERFECT* j'écrivais, tu écrivais, il/elle écrivait, nous écrivions, vous écriviez, ils/elles écrivaient

4. *PAST HISTORIC* j'écrivis, tu écrivis, il/elle écrivit, nous écrivîmes, vous écrivîtes, ils/elles écrivirent

5. *FUTURE* j'écrirai, tu écriras, il/elle écrira, nous écrirons, vous écrirez, ils/elles écriront

6. *CONDITIONAL* j'écrirais, tu écrirais, il/elle écrirait, nous écririons, vous écririez, ils/elles écriraient

7. *PAST PARTICIPLE* écrit

8. *PRESENT PARTICIPLE* écrivant

effrayer (*to frighten*) conjugation like 'donner' (i.e. regular), but in some tenses subject to predictable spelling changes: see VERB FORMS

emmener (*to take*) conjugation like 'donner' (i.e. regular), but in some tenses subject to predictable spelling changes: see VERB FORMS

employer (*to use*) conjugation like 'donner' (i.e. regular), but in some tenses subject to predictable spelling changes: see VERB FORMS

48 IRREGULAR VERBS

encourager (*to encourage*) conjugation like 'donner' (i.e. regular), but in some tenses subject to predictable spelling changes: see VERB FORMS

enlever (*to remove*) conjugation like 'donner' (i.e. regular), but in some tenses subject to predictable spelling changes: see VERB FORMS

ennuyer (*to bore*) conjugation like 'donner' (i.e. regular), but in some tenses subject to predictable spelling changes: see VERB FORMS

entreprendre (*to undertake*) conjugation *see* **prendre**

entretenir (*to maintain*) conjugation *see* **tenir**

entrevoir (*to make out*) conjugation *see* **voir**

envoyer (*to send*) auxiliary 'avoir': j'ai envoyé *etc*
1. *PRESENT* j'envoie, tu envoies, il/elle envoie, nous envoyons, vous envoyez, ils/elles envoient
2. *PRESENT SUBJUNCTIVE* j'envoie, tu envoies, il/elle envoie, nous envoyions, vous envoyiez, ils/elles envoient
3. *IMPERFECT* j'envoyais, tu envoyais, il/elle envoyait, nous envoyions, vous envoyiez, ils/elles envoyaient
4. *PAST HISTORIC* j'envoyai, tu envoyas, il/elle envoya, nous envoyâmes, vous envoyâtes, ils/elles envoyèrent
5. *FUTURE* j'enverrai, tu enverras, il/elle enverra, nous enverrons, vous enverrez, ils/elles enverront
6. *CONDITIONAL* j'enverrais, tu enverrais, il/elle enverrait, nous enverrions, vous enverriez, ils/elles enverraient
7. *PAST PARTICIPLE* envoyé
8. *PRESENT PARTICIPLE* envoyant

espérer (*to hope*) conjugation like 'donner' (i.e. regular), but in some tenses subject to predictable spelling changes: see VERB FORMS

essayer (*to try*) conjugation like 'donner' (i.e. regular), but in some tenses subject to predictable spelling changes: see VERB FORMS

IRREGULAR VERBS 49

essuyer (*to wipe*) conjugation like 'donner' (i.e. regular), but in some tenses subject to predictable spelling changes: see VERB FORMS

éteindre (*to switch off*) conjugation *see* **teindre**

être (*to be*) auxiliary 'avoir': j'ai été *etc*

1. *PRESENT* je suis, tu es, il/elle est, nous sommes, vous êtes, ils/elles sont

2. *PRESENT SUBJUNCTIVE* je sois, tu sois, il/elle soit, nous soyons, vous soyez, ils/elles soient

3. *IMPERFECT* j'étais, tu étais, il/elle était, nous étions, vous étiez, ils/elles étaient

4. *PAST HISTORIC* je fus, tu fus, il/elle fut, nous fûmes, vous fûtes, ils/elles furent

5. *FUTURE* je serai, tu seras, il/elle sera, nous serons, vous serez, ils/elles seront

6. *CONDITIONAL* je serais, tu serais, il/elle serait, nous serions, vous seriez, ils/elles seraient

7. *PAST PARTICIPLE* été

8. *PRESENT PARTICIPLE* étant

exclure (*to exclude*) conjugation *see* **conclure**

extraire (*to extract*) auxiliary 'avoir': j'ai extrait *etc*

1. *PRESENT* j'extrais, tu extrais, il/elle extrait, nous extrayons, vous extrayez, ils/elles extraient

2. *PRESENT SUBJUNCTIVE* j'extraie, tu extraies, il/elle extraie, nous extrayions, vous extrayiez, ils/elles extraient

3. *IMPERFECT* j'extrayais, tu extrayais, il/elle extrayait, nous extrayions, vous extrayiez, ils/elles extrayaient

4. *PAST HISTORIC not in current use*

5. *FUTURE* j'extrairai, tu extrairas, il/elle extraira, nous extrairons, vous extrairez, ils/elles extrairont

6. *CONDITIONAL* j'extrairais, tu extrairais, il/elle extrairait, nous extrairions, vous extrairiez, ils/elles extrairaient

7. *PAST PARTICIPLE* extrait

8. *PRESENT PARTICIPLE* extrayant

faillir *only in the perfect with the sense of 'nearly, almost...'*: j'ai failli tomber, tu as failli tomber *etc* *in the sense of 'fail', conjugation like 'finir' (regular,* *see* VERB FORMS): je faillis à ma tâche, nous faillissons *etc*

faire (*to do, make*) auxiliary 'avoir': j'ai fait *etc*
1. *PRESENT* je fais, tu fais, il/elle fait, nous faisons, vous faites, ils/elles font
2. *PRESENT SUBJUNCTIVE* je fasse, tu fasses, il/elle fasse, nous fassions, vous fassiez, ils/elles fassent
3. *IMPERFECT* je faisais, tu faisais, il/elle faisait, nous faisions, vous faisiez, ils/elles faisaient
4. *PAST HISTORIC* je fis, tu fis, il/elle fit, nous fîmes, vous fîtes, ils/elles firent
5. *FUTURE* je ferai, tu feras, il/elle fera, nous ferons, vous ferez, ils/elles feront
6. *CONDITIONAL* je ferais, tu ferais, il/elle ferait, nous ferions, vous feriez, ils/elles feraient
7. *PAST PARTICIPLE* fait
8. *PRESENT PARTICIPLE* faisant

falloir (*to be necessary*) 3rd person singular only, auxiliary 'avoir': il a fallu *etc*
1. *PRESENT* il faut
2. *PRESENT SUBJUNCTIVE* il faille
3. *IMPERFECT* il fallait
4. *PAST HISTORIC* il fallut
5. *FUTURE* il faudra
6. *CONDITIONAL* il faudrait
7. *PAST PARTICIPLE* fallu
8. *PRESENT PARTICIPLE* not in current use

feindre (*to pretend*) conjugation *see* **teindre**

forcer (*to force*) conjugation like 'donner' (i.e. regular), but in some tenses subject to predictable spelling changes: see VERB FORMS

frire (*to fry*) conjugation *see* **suffire**, except:
7. *PAST PARTICIPLE* frit

fuir (*to run away*) auxiliary 'avoir': j'ai fui *etc*
1. *PRESENT* je fuis, tu fuis, il/elle fuit, nous fuyons, vous fuyez, ils/elles fuient
2. *PRESENT SUBJUNCTIVE* je fuie, tu fuies, il/elle fuie, nous fuyions, vous fuyiez, ils/elles fuient

3. *IMPERFECT* je fuyais, tu fuyais, il/elle fuyait, nous fuyions, vous fuyiez, ils/elles fuyaient

4. *PAST HISTORIC* je fuis, tu fuis, il/elle fuit, nous fuîmes, vous fuîtes, ils/elles fuirent

5. *FUTURE* je fuirai, tu fuiras, il/elle fuira, nous fuirons, vous fuirez, ils/elles fuiront

6. *CONDITIONAL* je fuirais, tu fuirais, il/elle fuirait, nous fuirions, vous fuiriez, ils/elles fuiraient

7. *PAST PARTICIPLE* fui

8. *PRESENT PARTICIPLE* fuyant

geler (*to freeze*) conjugation like 'donner' (i.e. regular), but in some tenses subject to predictable spelling changes: see VERB FORMS

grincer (*to grate*) conjugation like 'donner' (i.e. regular), but in some tenses subject to predictable spelling changes: see VERB FORMS

haïr (*to hate*) auxiliary 'avoir': j'ai haï *etc*

1. *PRESENT* je hais, tu hais, il/elle hait, nous haïssons, vous haïssez, ils/elles haïssent

2. *PRESENT SUBJUNCTIVE* je haïsse, tu haïsses, il/elle haïsse, nous haïssions, vous haïssiez, ils/elles haïssent

3. *IMPERFECT* je haïssais, tu haïssais, il/elle haïssait, nous haïssions, vous haïssiez, ils/elles haïssaient

4. *PAST HISTORIC* je haïs, tu haïs, il/elle haït, nous haïmes, vous haïtes, ils/elles haïrent

5. *FUTURE* je haïrai, tu haïras, il/elle haïra, nous haïrons, vous haïrez, ils/elles haïront

6. *CONDITIONAL* je haïrais, tu haïrais, il/elle haïrait, nous haïrions, vous haïriez, ils/elles haïraient

7. *PAST PARTICIPLE* haï

8. *PRESENT PARTICIPLE* haïssant

inclure (*to enclose*) conjugation *see* **conclure**, except:

7. *PAST PARTICIPLE* inclus

influencer (*to influence*) conjugation like 'donner' (i.e. regular), but in some tenses subject to predictable spelling changes: see VERB FORMS

inquiéter (*to disturb*) conjugation like 'donner' (i.e. regular), but in some tenses subject to predictable spelling changes: see VERB FORMS

inscrire (*to write down*) conjugation *see* **écrire**

instruire (*to teach*) conjugation *see* **cuire**

interdire (*to forbid*) conjugation *see* **dire**, except for:
1. *PRESENT* j'interdis, tu interdis, il/elle interdit, nous interdisons, vous interdisez, ils/elles interdisent

interroger (*to ask*) conjugation like 'donner' (i.e. regular), but in some tenses subject to predictable spelling changes: see VERB FORMS

introduire (*to insert*) conjugation *see* **cuire**

jeter (*to throw*) conjugation like 'donner' (i.e. regular), but in some tenses subject to predictable spelling changes: see VERB FORMS

joindre (*to join*) auxiliary 'avoir': j'ai joint *etc*
1. *PRESENT* je joins, tu joins, il/elle joint, nous joignons, vous joignez, ils/elles joignent
2. *PRESENT SUBJUNCTIVE* je joigne, tu joignes, il/elle joigne, nous joignions, vous joigniez, ils/elles joignent
3. *IMPERFECT* je joignais, tu joignais, il/elle joignait, nous joignions, vous joigniez, ils/elles joignaient
4. *PAST HISTORIC* je joignis, tu joignis, il/elle joignit, nous joignîmes, vous joignîtes, ils/elles joignirent
5. *FUTURE* je joindrai, tu joindras, il/elle joindra, nous joindrons, vous joindrez, ils/elles joindront
6. *CONDITIONAL* je joindrais, tu joindrais, il/elle joindrait, nous joindrions, vous joindriez, ils/elles joindraient
7. *PAST PARTICIPLE* joint
8. *PRESENT PARTICIPLE* joignant

juger (*to judge*) conjugation like 'donner' (i.e. regular), but in some tenses subject to predictable spelling changes: see VERB FORMS

IRREGULAR VERBS

lancer (*to throw*) conjugation like 'donner' (i.e. regular), but in some tenses subject to predictable spelling changes: see VERB FORMS

lever (*to raise*) conjugation like 'donner' (i.e. regular), but in some tenses subject to predictable spelling changes: see VERB FORMS

lire (*to read*) auxiliary 'avoir': j'ai lu *etc*
1. *PRESENT* je lis, tu lis, il/elle lit, nous lisons, vous lisez, ils/elles lisent
2. *PRESENT SUBJUNCTIVE* je lise, tu lises, il/elle lise, nous lisions, vous lisiez, ils/elles lisent
3. *IMPERFECT* je lisais, tu lisais, il/elle lisait, nous lisions, vous lisiez, ils/elles lisaient
4. *PAST HISTORIC* je lus, tu lus, il/elle lut, nous lûmes, vous lûtes, ils/elles lurent
5. *FUTURE* je lirai, tu liras, il/elle lira, nous lirons, vous lirez, ils/elles liront
6. *CONDITIONAL* je lirais, tu lirais, il/elle lirait, nous lirions, vous liriez, ils/elles liraient
7. *PAST PARTICIPLE* lu
8. *PRESENT PARTICIPLE* lisant

loger (*to stay*) conjugation like 'donner' (i.e. regular), but in some tenses subject to predictable spelling changes: see VERB FORMS

luire (*to shine*) conjugation *see* **cuire** except:
7. *PAST PARTICIPLE* lui

maintenir (*to maintain*) conjugation *see* **tenir**

manger (*to eat*) conjugation like 'donner' (i.e. regular), but in some tenses subject to predictable spelling changes: see VERB FORMS

menacer (*to threaten*) conjugation like 'donner' (i.e. regular), but in some tenses subject to predictable spelling changes: see VERB FORMS

mener (*to lead*) conjugation like 'donner' (i.e. regular), but in some tenses subject to predictable spelling changes: see VERB FORMS

mentir (*to lie*) conjugation *see* **sentir**

mettre (*to put*) auxiliary 'avoir': j'ai mis *etc*

1. *PRESENT* je mets, tu mets, il/elle met, nous mettons, vous mettez, ils/elles mettent

2. *PRESENT SUBJUNCTIVE* je mette, tu mettes, il/elle mette, nous mettions, vous mettiez, ils/elles mettent

3. *IMPERFECT* je mettais, tu mettais, il/elle mettait, nous mettions, vous mettiez, ils/elles mettaient

4. *PAST HISTORIC* je mis, tu mis, il/elle mit, nous mîmes, vous mîtes, ils/elles mirent

5. *FUTURE* je mettrai, tu mettras, il/elle mettra, nous mettrons, vous mettrez, ils/elles mettront

6. *CONDITIONAL* je mettrais, tu mettrais, il/elle mettrait, nous mettrions, vous mettriez, ils/elles mettraient

7. *PAST PARTICIPLE* mis

8. *PRESENT PARTICIPLE* mettant

mordre (*to bite*) auxiliary 'avoir': j'ai mordu *etc*

1. *PRESENT* je mords, tu mords, il/elle mord, nous mordons, vous mordez, ils/elles mordent

2. *PRESENT SUBJUNCTIVE* je morde, tu mordes, il/elle morde, nous mordions, vous mordiez, ils/elles mordent

3. *IMPERFECT* je mordais, tu mordais, il/elle mordait, nous mordions, vous mordiez, ils/elles mordaient

4. *PAST HISTORIC* je mordis, tu mordis, il/elle mordit, nous mordîmes, vous mordîtes, ils/elles mordirent

5. *FUTURE* je mordrai, tu mordras, il/elle mordra, nous mordrons, vous mordrez, ils/elles mordront

6. *CONDITIONAL* je mordrais, tu mordrais, il/elle mordrait, nous mordrions, vous mordriez, ils/elles mordraient

7. *PAST PARTICIPLE* mordu

8. *PRESENT PARTICIPLE* mordant

moudre (*to grind*) auxiliary 'avoir': j'ai moulu *etc*

1. *PRESENT* je mouds, tu mouds, il/elle moud, nous moulons, vous moulez, ils/elles moulent

2. *PRESENT SUBJUNCTIVE* je moule, tu moules, il/elle moule, nous moulions, vous mouliez, ils/elles moulent

IRREGULAR VERBS

3. *IMPERFECT* je moulais, tu moulais, il/elle moulait, nous moulions, vous mouliez, ils/elles moulaient

4. *PAST HISTORIC* je moulus, tu moulus, il/elle moulut, nous moulûmes, vous moulûtes, ils/elles moulurent

5. *FUTURE* je moudrai, tu moudras, il/elle moudra, nous moudrons, vous moudrez, ils/elles moudront

6. *CONDITIONAL* je moudrais, tu moudrais, il/elle moudrait, nous moudrions, vous moudriez, ils/elles moudraient

7. *PAST PARTICIPLE* moulu

8. *PRESENT PARTICIPLE* moulant

mourir (*to die*) auxiliary 'être': je suis mort *etc*

1. *PRESENT* je meurs, tu meurs, il/elle meurt, nous mourons, vous mourez, ils/elles meurent

2. *PRESENT SUBJUNCTIVE* je meure, tu meures, il/elle meure, nous mourions, vous mouriez, ils/elles meurent

3. *IMPERFECT* je mourais, tu mourais, il/elle mourait, nous mourions, vous mouriez, ils/elles mouraient

4. *PAST HISTORIC* je mourus, tu mourus, il/elle mourut, nous mourûmes, vous mourûtes, ils/elles moururent

5. *FUTURE* je mourrai, tu mourras, il/elle mourra, nous mourrons, vous mourrez, ils/elles mourront

6. *CONDITIONAL* je mourrais, tu mourrais, il/elle mourrait, nous mourrions, vous mourriez, ils/elles mourraient

7. *PAST PARTICIPLE* mort

8. *PRESENT PARTICIPLE* mourant

se mouvoir (*to move*) auxiliary 'être': je me suis mû *etc*

1. *PRESENT* je me meus, tu te meus, il/elle se meut, nous nous mouvons, vous vous mouvez, ils/elles se meuvent

2. *PRESENT SUBJUNCTIVE* je me meuve, tu te meuves, il/elle se meuve, nous nous mouvions, vous vous mouviez, ils/elles se meuvent

3. *IMPERFECT* je me mouvais, tu te mouvais, il/elle

56 IRREGULAR VERBS

se mouvait, nous nous mouvions, vous vous mouviez, ils/elles se mouvaient

4. *PAST HISTORIC* je me mus, tu te mus, il/elle se mut, nous nous mûmes, vous vous mûtes, ils/elles se murent

5. *FUTURE* je me mouvrai, tu te mouvras, il/elle se mouvra, nous nous mouvrons, vous vous mouvrez, ils/elles se mouvront

6. *CONDITIONAL* je me mouvrais, tu te mouvrais, il/elle se mouvrait, nous nous mouvrions, vous vous mouvriez, ils/elles se mouvraient

7. *PAST PARTICIPLE* mû

8. *PRESENT PARTICIPLE* se mouvant

nager (*to swim*) conjugation like 'donner' (i.e. regular), but in some tenses subject to predictable spelling changes: see VERB FORMS

naître (*to be born*) auxiliary 'être': je suis né *etc*

1. *PRESENT* je nais, tu nais, il/elle naît, nous naissons, vous naissez, ils/elles naissent

2. *PRESENT SUBJUNCTIVE* je naisse, tu naisses, il/elle naisse, nous naissions, vous naissiez, ils/elles naissent

3. *IMPERFECT* je naissais, tu naissais, il/elle naissait, nous naissions, vous naissiez, ils/elles naissaient

4. *PAST HISTORIC* je naquis, tu naquis, il/elle naquit, nous naquîmes, vous naquîtes, ils/elles naquirent

5. *FUTURE* je naîtrai, tu naîtras, il/elle naîtra, nous naîtrons, vous naîtrez, ils/elles naîtront

6. *CONDITIONAL* je naîtrais, tu naîtrais, il/elle naîtrait, nous naîtrions, vous naîtriez, ils/elles naîtraient

7. *PAST PARTICIPLE* né

8. *PRESENT PARTICIPLE* naissant

neiger (*to snow*) conjugation like 'donner' (i.e. regular), but in some tenses subject to predictable spelling changes: see VERB FORMS

nettoyer (*to clean*) conjugation like 'donner' (i.e. regular), but in some tenses subject to predictable

IRREGULAR VERBS 57

spelling changes: see VERB FORMS

se noyer (*to drown*) conjugation like 'donner' (i.e. regular), but in some tenses subject to predictable spelling changes: see VERB FORMS

nuire (*to damage*) conjugation *see* **cuire** except:
7. *PAST PARTICIPLE* nui

obliger (*to force*) conjugation like 'donner' (i.e. regular), but in some tenses subject to predictable spelling changes: see VERB FORMS

obtenir (*to get*) conjugation *see* **tenir**

offrir (*to offer*) auxiliary 'avoir': j'ai offert *etc*
1. *PRESENT* j'offre, tu offres, il/elle offre, nous offrons, vous offrez, ils/elles offrent
2. *PRESENT SUBJUNCTIVE* j'offre, tu offres, il/elle offre, nous offrions, vous offriez, ils/elles offrent
3. *IMPERFECT* j'offrais, tu offrais, il/elle offrait, nous offrions, vous offriez, ils/elles offraient
4. *PAST HISTORIC* j'offris, tu offris, il/elle offrit, nous offrîmes, vous offrîtes, ils/elles offrirent
5. *FUTURE* j'offrirai, tu offriras, il/elle offrira, nous offrirons, vous offrirez, ils/elles offriront
6. *CONDITIONAL* j'offrirais, tu offrirais, il/elle offrirait, nous offririons, vous offririez, ils/elles offriraient
7. *PAST PARTICIPLE* offert
8. *PRESENT PARTICIPLE* offrant

omettre (*to omit*) conjugation *see* **mettre**

ouvrir (*to open*) conjugation *see* **couvrir**

paraître (*to appear*) auxiliary 'avoir': j'ai paru *etc*
1. *PRESENT* je parais, tu parais, il/elle paraît, nous paraissons, vous paraissez, ils/elles paraissent
2. *PRESENT SUBJUNCTIVE* je paraisse, tu paraisses, il/elle paraisse, nous paraissions, vous paraissiez, ils/elles paraissent
3. *IMPERFECT* je paraissais, tu paraissais, il/elle paraissait, nous paraissions, vous paraissiez, ils/elles paraissaient
4. *PAST HISTORIC* je parus, tu parus, il/elle parut, nous parûmes, vous parûtes, ils/elles parurent

IRREGULAR VERBS

5. *FUTURE* je paraîtrai, tu paraîtras, il/elle paraîtra, nous paraîtrons, vous paraîtrez, ils/elles paraîtront

6. *CONDITIONAL* je paraîtrais, tu paraîtrais, il/elle paraîtrait, nous paraîtrions, vous paraîtriez, ils/elles paraîtraient

7. *PAST PARTICIPLE* paru

8. *PRESENT PARTICIPLE* paraissant

partager (*to share*) conjugation like 'donner' (i.e. regular), but in some tenses subject to predictable spelling changes: see VERB FORMS

partir (*to leave*) auxiliary 'être': je suis parti *etc*
1. *PRESENT* je pars, tu pars, il/elle part, nous partons, vous partez, ils/elles partent

2. *PRESENT SUBJUNCTIVE* je parte, tu partes, il/elle parte, nous partions, vous partiez, ils/elles partent

3. *IMPERFECT* je partais, tu partais, il/elle partait, nous partions, vous partiez, ils/elles partaient

4. *PAST HISTORIC* je partis, tu partis, il/elle partit, nous partîmes, vous partîtes, ils/elles partirent

5. *FUTURE* je partirai, tu partiras, il/elle partira, nous partirons, vous partirez, ils/elles partiront

6. *CONDITIONAL* je partirais, tu partirais, il/elle partirait, nous partirions, vous partiriez, ils/elles partiraient

7. *PAST PARTICIPLE* parti

8. *PRESENT PARTICIPLE* partant

payer (*to pay*) conjugation like 'donner' (i.e. regular), but in some tenses subject to predictable spelling changes: see VERB FORMS

peindre (*to paint*) conjugation *see* **teindre**

permettre (*to allow*) conjugation *see* **mettre**

peser (*to weigh*) conjugation like 'donner' (i.e. regular), but in some tenses subject to predictable spelling changes: see VERB FORMS

placer (*to put*) conjugation like 'donner' (i.e. regular), but in some tenses subject to predictable spelling changes: see VERB FORMS

plaindre (*to pity*) conjugation *see* **craindre**

plaire (*to please*) auxiliary 'avoir': j'ai plu *etc*
1. *PRESENT* je plais, tu plais, il/elle plaît, nous plaisons, vous plaisez, ils/elles plaisent
2. *PRESENT SUBJUNCTIVE* je plaise, tu plaises, il/elle plaise, nous plaisions, vous plaisiez, ils/elles plaisent
3. *IMPERFECT* je plaisais, tu plaisais, il/elle plaisait, nous plaisions, vous plaisiez, ils/elles plaisaient
4. *PAST HISTORIC* je plus, tu plus, il/elle plut, nous plûmes, vous plûtes, ils/elles plurent
5. *FUTURE* je plairai, tu plairas, il/elle plaira, nous plairons, vous plairez, ils/elles plairont
6. *CONDITIONAL* je plairais, tu plairais, il/elle plairait, nous plairions, vous plairiez, ils/elles plairaient
7. *PAST PARTICIPLE* plu
8. *PRESENT PARTICIPLE* plaisant

pleuvoir (*to rain*) auxiliary 'avoir': il a plu *etc*; impersonal or 3rd person only (in figurative sense)
1. *PRESENT* il pleut, ils/elles pleuvent
2. *PRESENT SUBJUNCTIVE* il pleuve, ils/elles pleuvent
3. *IMPERFECT* il pleuvait, ils/elles pleuvaient
4. *PAST HISTORIC* il plut, ils/elles plurent
5. *FUTURE* il pleuvra, ils/elles pleuvront
6. *CONDITIONAL* il pleuvrait, ils/elles pleuvraient
7. *PAST PARTICIPLE* plu
8. *PRESENT PARTICIPLE* pleuvant

plonger (*to dive*) conjugation like 'donner' (i.e. regular), but in some tenses subject to predictable spelling changes: see VERB FORMS

posséder (*to own*) conjugation like 'donner' (i.e. regular), but in some tenses subject to predictable spelling changes: see VERB FORMS

poursuivre (*to follow*) conjugation *see* **suivre**

pourvoir (*to provide*) auxiliary 'avoir': j'ai pourvu
1. *PRESENT* je pourvois, tu pourvois, il/elle pourvoit, nous pourvoyons, vous pourvoyez, ils/elles pourvoient

60 IRREGULAR VERBS

2. *PRESENT SUBJUNCTIVE* je pourvoie, tu pourvoies, il/elle pourvoie, nous pourvoyions, vous pourvoyiez, ils/elles pourvoient

3. *IMPERFECT* je pourvoyais, tu pourvoyais, il/elle pourvoyait, nous pourvoyions, vous pourvoyiez, ils/elles pourvoyaient

4. *PAST HISTORIC* je pourvus, tu pourvus, il/elle pourvut, nous pourvûmes, vous pourvûtes, ils/elles pourvurent

5. *FUTURE* je pourvoirai, tu pourvoiras, il/elle pourvoira, nous pourvoirons, vous pourvoirez, ils/elles pourvoiront

6. *CONDITIONAL* je pourvoirais, tu pourvoirais, il/elle pourvoirait, nous pourvoirions, vous pourvoiriez, ils/elles pourvoiraient

7. *PAST PARTICIPLE* pourvu

8. *PRESENT PARTICIPLE* pourvoyant

pouvoir (*to be able to*) auxiliary 'avoir': j'ai pu *etc*

1. *PRESENT* je peux, tu peux, il/elle peut, nous pouvons, vous pouvez, ils/elles peuvent

2. *PRESENT SUBJUNCTIVE* je puisse, tu puisses, il/elle puisse, nous puissions, vous puissiez, ils/elles puissent

3. *IMPERFECT* je pouvais, tu pouvais, il/elle pouvait, nous pouvions, vous pouviez, ils/elles pouvaient

4. *PAST HISTORIC* je pus, tu pus, il/elle put, nous pûmes, vous pûtes, ils/elles purent

5. *FUTURE* je pourrai, tu pourras, il/elle pourra, nous pourrons, vous pourrez, ils/elles pourront

6. *CONDITIONAL* je pourrais, tu pourrais, il/elle pourrait, nous pourrions, vous pourriez, ils/elles pourraient

7. *PAST PARTICIPLE* pu

8. *PRESENT PARTICIPLE* pouvant

préférer (*to prefer*) conjugation like 'donner' (i.e. regular), but in some tenses subject to predictable spelling changes: see VERB FORMS

prendre (*to take*) auxiliary 'avoir': j'ai pris *etc*

1. *PRESENT* je prends, tu prends, il/elle prend, nous prenons, vous prenez, ils/elles prennent

IRREGULAR VERBS

2. *PRESENT SUBJUNCTIVE* je prenne, tu prennes, il/elle prenne, nous prenions, vous preniez, ils/elles prennent

3. *IMPERFECT* je prenais, tu prenais, il/elle prenait, nous prenions, vous preniez, ils/elles prenaient

4. *PAST HISTORIC* je pris, tu pris, il/elle prit, nous prîmes, vous prîtes, ils/elles prirent

5. *FUTURE* je prendrai, tu prendras, il/elle prendra, nous prendrons, vous prendrez, ils/elles prendront

6. *CONDITIONAL* je prendrais, tu prendrais, il/elle prendrait, nous prendrions, vous prendriez, ils/elles prendraient

7. *PAST PARTICIPLE* pris

8. *PRESENT PARTICIPLE* prenant

prévenir (*to warn*) conjugation *see* **venir** but auxiliary 'avoir': j'ai prévenu

prévoir (*to foresee*) conjugation *see* **voir** except for the following:

5. *FUTURE* je prévoirai, tu prévoiras, il/elle prévoira, nous prévoirons, vous prévoirez, ils/elles prévoiront

6. *CONDITIONAL* je prévoirais, tu prévoirais, il/elle prévoirait, nous prévoirions, vous prévoiriez, ils/elles prévoiraient

produire (*to produce*) conjugation *see* **cuire**

promettre (*to promise*) conjugation *see* **mettre**

protéger (*to protect*) conjugation like 'donner' (i.e. regular), but in some tenses subject to predictable spelling changes: see VERB FORMS

ranger (*to arrange*) conjugation like 'donner' (i.e. regular), but in some tenses subject to predictable spelling changes: see VERB FORMS

recevoir (*to receive*) auxiliary 'avoir': j'ai reçu *etc*

1. *PRESENT* je reçois, tu reçois, il/elle reçoit, nous recevons, vous recevez, ils/elles reçoivent

2. *PRESENT SUBJUNCTIVE* je reçoive, tu reçoives, il/elle reçoive, nous recevions, vous receviez, ils/elles reçoivent

3. *IMPERFECT* je recevais, tu recevais, il/elle

62 IRREGULAR VERBS

recevait, nous recevions, vous receviez, ils/elles recevaient

4. *PAST HISTORIC* je reçus, tu reçus, il/elle reçut, nous reçûmes, vous reçûtes, ils/elles reçurent

5. *FUTURE* je recevrai, tu recevras, il/elle recevra, nous recevrons, vous recevrez, ils/elles recevront

6. *CONDITIONAL* je recevrais, tu recevrais, il/elle recevrait, nous recevrions, vous recevriez, ils/elles recevraient

7. *PAST PARTICIPLE* reçu

8. *PRESENT PARTICIPLE* recevant

recommencer (*to start again*) conjugation like 'donner' (i.e. regular), but in some tenses subject to predictable spelling changes: see VERB FORMS

reconnaître (*to recognize*) conjugation *see* **connaître**

recouvrir (*to cover*) conjugation *see* **couvrir**

réduire (*to reduce*) conjugation *see* **cuire**

refléter (*to reflect*) conjugation like 'donner' (i.e. regular), but in some tenses subject to predictable spelling changes: see VERB FORMS

rejeter (*to reject*) conjugation like 'donner' (i.e. regular), but in some tenses subject to predictable spelling changes: see VERB FORMS

remplacer (*to replace*) conjugation like 'donner' (i.e. regular), but in some tenses subject to predictable spelling changes: see VERB FORMS

renvoyer (*to send back*) conjugation *see* **envoyer**

repartir (*to go again*) conjugation *see* **partir**

répéter (*to repeat*) conjugation like 'donner' (i.e. regular), but in some tenses subject to predictable spelling changes: see VERB FORMS

replacer (*to replace*) conjugation like 'donner' (i.e. regular), but in some tenses subject to predictable spelling changes: see VERB FORMS

répondre (*to reply*) auxiliary 'avoir': j'ai répondu

1. *PRESENT* je réponds, tu réponds, il/elle répond,

IRREGULAR VERBS

nous répondons, vous répondez, ils/elles répondent
2. *PRESENT SUBJUNCTIVE* je réponde, tu répondes, il/elle réponde, nous répondions, vous répondiez, ils/elles répondent
3. *IMPERFECT* je répondais, tu répondais, il/elle répondait, nous répondions, vous répondiez, ils/elles répondaient
4. *PAST HISTORIC* je répondis, tu répondis, il/elle répondit, nous répondîmes, vous répondîtes, ils/elles répondirent
5. *FUTURE* je répondrai, tu répondras, il/elle répondra, nous répondrons, vous répondrez, ils/elles répondront
6. *CONDITIONAL* je répondrais, tu répondrais, il/elle répondrait, nous répondrions, vous répondriez, ils/elles répondraient
7. *PAST PARTICIPLE* répondu
8. *PRESENT PARTICIPLE* répondant

reproduire (*to copy*) conjugation *see* **cuire**

résoudre (*to solve*) auxiliary 'avoir': j'ai résolu *etc*
1. *PRESENT* je résous, tu résous, il/elle résout, nous résolvons, vous résolvez, ils/elles résolvent
2. *PRESENT SUBJUNCTIVE* je résolve, tu résolves, il/elle résolve, nous résolvions, vous résolviez, ils/elles résolvent
3. *IMPERFECT* je résolvais, tu résolvais, il/elle résolvait, nous résolvions, vous résolviez, ils/elles résolvaient
4. *PAST HISTORIC* je résolus, tu résolus, il/elle résolut, nous résolûmes, vous résolûtes, ils/elles résolurent
5. *FUTURE* je résoudrai, tu résoudras, il/elle résoudra, nous résoudrons, vous résoudrez, ils/elles résoudront
6. *CONDITIONAL* je résoudrais, tu résoudrais, il/elle résoudrait, nous résoudrions, vous résoudriez, ils/elles résoudraient
7. *PAST PARTICIPLE* résolu
8. *PRESENT PARTICIPLE* résolvant

retenir (*to retain*) conjugation *see* **tenir**

revenir (*to come back*) conjugation *see* **venir**

revêtir (*to put on*) conjugation *see* **vêtir**

revoir (*to see again*) conjugation *see* **voir**

rire (*to laugh*) auxiliary 'avoir': j'ai ri *etc*

1. *PRESENT* je ris, tu ris, il/elle rit, nous rions, vous riez, ils/elles rient
2. *PRESENT SUBJUNCTIVE* je rie, tu ries, il/elle rie, nous riions, vous riiez, ils/elles rient
3. *IMPERFECT* je riais, tu riais, il/elle riait, nous riions, vous riiez, ils/elles riaient
4. *PAST HISTORIC* je ris, tu ris, il/elle rit, nous rîmes, vous rîtes, ils/elles rirent
5. *FUTURE* je rirai, tu riras, il/elle rira, nous rirons, vous rirez, ils/elles riront
6. *CONDITIONAL* je rirais, tu rirais, il/elle rirait, nous ririons, vous ririez, ils/elles riraient
7. *PAST PARTICIPLE* ri
8. *PRESENT PARTICIPLE* riant

rompre (*to break*) auxiliary 'avoir': j'ai rompu *etc*

1. *PRESENT* je romps, tu romps, il/elle rompt, nous rompons, vous rompez, ils/elles rompent
2. *PRESENT SUBJUNCTIVE* je rompe, tu rompes, il/elle rompe, nous rompions, vous rompiez, ils/elles rompent
3. *IMPERFECT* je rompais, tu rompais, il/elle rompait, nous rompions, vous rompiez, ils/elles rompaient
4. *PAST HISTORIC* je rompis, tu rompis, il/elle rompit, nous rompîmes, vous rompîtes, ils/elles rompirent
5. *FUTURE* je romprai, tu rompras, il/elle rompra, nous romprons, vous romprez, ils/elles rompront
6. *CONDITIONAL* je romprais, tu romprais, il/elle romprait, nous romprions, vous rompriez, ils/elles rompraient
7. *PAST PARTICIPLE* rompu
8. *PRESENT PARTICIPLE* rompant

satisfaire (*to satisfy*) conjugation *see* **faire**

savoir (*to know*) auxiliary 'avoir': j'ai su *etc*
1. *PRESENT* je sais, tu sais, il/elle sait, nous savons, vous savez, ils/elles savent
2. *PRESENT SUBJUNCTIVE* je sache, tu saches, il/elle sache, nous sachions, vous sachiez, ils/elles sachent
3. *IMPERFECT* je savais, tu savais, il/elle savait, nous savions, vous saviez, ils/elles savaient
4. *PAST HISTORIC* je sus, tu sus, il/elle sut, nous sûmes, vous sûtes, ils/elles surent
5. *FUTURE* je saurai, tu sauras, il/elle saura, nous saurons, vous saurez, ils/elles sauront
6. *CONDITIONAL* je saurais, tu saurais, il/elle saurait, nous saurions, vous sauriez, ils/elles sauraient
7. *PAST PARTICIPLE* su
8. *PRESENT PARTICIPLE* sachant

sécher (*to dry*) conjugation like 'donner' (i.e. regular), but in some tenses subject to predictable spelling changes: see VERB FORMS

sentir (*to smell, feel*) auxiliary 'avoir': j'ai senti *etc*
1. *PRESENT* je sens, tu sens, il/elle sent, nous sentons, vous sentez, ils/elles sentent
2. *PRESENT SUBJUNCTIVE* je sente, tu sentes, il/elle sente, nous sentions, vous sentiez, ils/elles sentent
3. *IMPERFECT* je sentais, tu sentais, il/elle sentait, nous sentions, vous sentiez, ils/elles sentaient
4. *PAST HISTORIC* je sentis, tu sentis, il/elle sentit, nous sentîmes, vous sentîtes, ils/elles sentirent
5. *FUTURE* je sentirai, tu sentiras, il/elle sentira, nous sentirons, vous sentirez, ils/elles sentiront
6. *CONDITIONAL* je sentirais, tu sentirais, il/elle sentirait, nous sentirions, vous sentiriez, ils/elles sentiraient
7. *PAST PARTICIPLE* senti
8. *PRESENT PARTICIPLE* sentant

servir (*to serve*) auxiliary 'avoir': j'ai servi *etc*
1. *PRESENT* je sers, tu sers, il/elle sert, nous servons, vous servez, ils/elles servent
2. *PRESENT SUBJUNCTIVE* je serve, tu serves, il/elle

66 IRREGULAR VERBS

serve, nous servions, vous serviez, ils/elles servent

3. *IMPERFECT* je servais, tu servais, il/elle servait, nous servions, vous serviez, ils/elles servaient

4. *PAST HISTORIC* je servis, tu servis, il/elle servit, nous servîmes, vous servîtes, ils/elles servirent

5. *FUTURE* je servirai, tu serviras, il/elle servira, nous servirons, vous servirez, ils/elles serviront

6. *CONDITIONAL* je servirais, tu servirais, il/elle servirait, nous servirions, vous serviriez, ils/elles serviraient

7. *PAST PARTICIPLE* servi

8. *PRESENT PARTICIPLE* servant

songer (*to dream*) conjugation like 'donner' (i.e. regular), but in some tenses subject to predictable spelling changes: see VERB FORMS

sortir (*to go out*) auxiliary 'être': je suis sorti *etc*

1. *PRESENT* je sors, tu sors, il/elle sort, nous sortons, vous sortez, ils/elles sortent

2. *PRESENT SUBJUNCTIVE* je sorte, tu sortes, il/elle sorte, nous sortions, vous sortiez, ils/elles sortent

3. *IMPERFECT* je sortais, tu sortais, il/elle sortait, nous sortions, vous sortiez, ils/elles sortaient

4. *PAST HISTORIC* je sortis, tu sortis, il/elle sortit, nous sortîmes, vous sortîtes, ils/elles sortirent

5. *FUTURE* je sortirai, tu sortiras, il/elle sortira, nous sortirons, vous sortirez, ils/elles sortiront

6. *CONDITIONAL* je sortirais, tu sortirais, il/elle sortirait, nous sortirions, vous sortiriez, ils/elles sortiraient

7. *PAST PARTICIPLE* sorti

8. *PRESENT PARTICIPLE* sortant

souffrir (*to suffer*) conjugation *see* **couvrir**

sourire (*to smile*) conjugation *see* **rire**

soutenir (*to hold*) conjugation *see* **tenir**

se souvenir (*to remember*) conjugation *see* **venir**

suffire (*to be enough*) auxiliary 'avoir': j'ai suffi *etc*

1. *PRESENT* je suffis, tu suffis, il/elle suffit, nous suffisons, vous suffisez, ils/elles suffisent

2. *PRESENT SUBJUNCTIVE* je suffise, tu suffises,

IRREGULAR VERBS

il/elle suffise, nous suffisions, vous suffisiez, ils/elles suffisent

3. *IMPERFECT* je suffisais, tu suffisais, il/elle suffisait, nous suffisions, vous suffisiez, ils/elles suffisaient

4. *PAST HISTORIC* je suffis, tu suffis, il/elle suffit, nous suffîmes, vous suffîtes, ils/elles suffirent

5. *FUTURE* je suffirai, tu suffiras, il/elle suffira, nous suffirons, vous suffirez, ils/elles suffiront

6. *CONDITIONAL* je suffirais, tu suffirais, il/elle suffirait, nous suffirions, vous suffiriez, ils/elles suffiraient

7. *PAST PARTICIPLE* suffi

8. *PRESENT PARTICIPLE* suffisant

suivre (*to follow*) auxiliary 'avoir': j'ai suivi *etc*

1. *PRESENT* je suis, tu suis, il/elle suit, nous suivons, vous suivez, ils/elles suivent

2. *PRESENT SUBJUNCTIVE* je suive, tu suives, il/elle suive, nous suivions, vous suiviez, ils/elles suivent

3. *IMPERFECT* je suivais, tu suivais, il/elle suivait, nous suivions, vous suiviez, ils/elles suivaient

4. *PAST HISTORIC* je suivis, tu suivis, il/elle suivit, nous suivîmes, vous suivîtes, ils/elles suivirent

5. *FUTURE* je suivrai, tu suivras, il/elle suivra, nous suivrons, vous suivrez, ils/elles suivront

6. *CONDITIONAL* je suivrais, tu suivrais, il/elle suivrait, nous suivrions, vous suivriez, ils/elles suivraient

7. *PAST PARTICIPLE* suivi

8. *PRESENT PARTICIPLE* suivant

se taire (*to keep silent*) auxiliary 'être': je me suis tu

1. *PRESENT* je me tais, tu te tais, il/elle se tait, nous nous taisons, vous vous taisez, ils/elles se taisent

2. *PRESENT SUBJUNCTIVE* je me taise, tu te taises, il/elle se taise, nous nous taisions, vous vous taisiez, ils/elles se taisent

3. *IMPERFECT* je me taisais, tu te taisais, il/elle se taisait, nous nous taisions, vous vous taisiez, ils/elles se taisaient

4. *PAST HISTORIC* je me tus, tu te tus, il/elle se tut,

68 IRREGULAR VERBS

nous nous tûmes, vous vous tûtes, ils/elles se turent

5. *FUTURE* je me tairai, tu te tairas, il/elle se taira, nous nous tairons, vous vous tairez, ils/elles se tairont

6. *CONDITIONAL* je me tairais, tu te tairais, il/elle se tairait, nous nous tairions, vous vous tairiez, ils/elles se tairaient

7. *PAST PARTICIPLE* tu

8. *PRESENT PARTICIPLE* se taisant

teindre (*to dye*) auxiliary 'avoir': j'ai teint *etc*

1. *PRESENT* je teins, tu teins, il/elle teint, nous teignons, vous teignez, ils/elles teignent

2. *PRESENT SUBJUNCTIVE* je teigne, tu teignes, il/elle teigne, nous teignions, vous teigniez, ils/elles teignent

3. *IMPERFECT* je teignais, tu teignais, il/elle teignait, nous teignions, vous teigniez, ils/elles teignaient

4. *PAST HISTORIC* je teignis, tu teignis, il/elle teignit, nous teignîmes, vous teignîtes, ils/elles teignirent

5. *FUTURE* je teindrai, tu teindras, il/elle teindra, nous teindrons, vous teindrez, ils/elles teindront

6. *CONDITIONAL* je teindrais, tu teindrais, il/elle teindrait, nous teindrions, vous teindriez, ils/elles teindraient

7. *PAST PARTICIPLE* teint

8. *PRESENT PARTICIPLE* teignant

tenir (*to hold*) auxiliary 'avoir': j'ai tenu *etc*

1. *PRESENT* je tiens, tu tiens, il/elle tient, nous tenons, vous tenez, ils/elles tiennent

2. *PRESENT SUBJUNCTIVE* je tienne, tu tiennes, il/elle tienne, nous tenions, vous teniez, ils/elles tiennent

3. *IMPERFECT* je tenais, tu tenais, il/elle tenait, nous tenions, vous teniez, ils/elles tenaient

4. *PAST HISTORIC* je tins, tu tins, il/elle tint, nous tînmes, vous tîntes, ils tinrent

5. *FUTURE* je tiendrai, tu tiendras, il/elle tiendra, nous tiendrons, vous tiendrez, ils/elles tiendront

6. *CONDITIONAL* je tiendrais, tu tiendrais, il/elle

tiendrait, nous tiendrions, vous tiendriez, ils/elles tiendraient

7. *PAST PARTICIPLE* tenu

8. *PRESENT PARTICIPLE* tenant

traduire (*to translate*) conjugation *see* **cuire**

vaincre (*to defeat*) auxiliary 'avoir': j'ai vaincu *etc*

1. *PRESENT* je vaincs, tu vaincs, il/elle vainc, nous vainquons, vous vainquez, ils/elles vainquent

2. *PRESENT SUBJUNCTIVE* je vainque, tu vainques, il vainque, nous vainquions, vous vainquiez, ils/elles vainquent

3. *IMPERFECT* je vainquais, tu vainquais, il/elle vainquait, nous vainquions, vous vainquiez, ils/elles vainquaient

4. *PAST HISTORIC* je vainquis, tu vainquis, il/elle vainquit, nous vainquîmes, vous vainquîtes, ils/elles vainquirent

5. *FUTURE* je vaincrai, tu vaincras, il/elle vaincra, nous vaincrons, vous vaincrez, ils/elles vaincront

6. *CONDITIONAL* je vaincrais, tu vaincrais, il/elle vaincrait, nous vaincrions, vous vaincriez, ils/elles vaincraient

7. *PAST PARTICIPLE* vaincu

8. *PRESENT PARTICIPLE* vainquant

valoir (*to be worth*) auxiliary 'avoir': j'ai valu *etc*

1. *PRESENT* je vaux, tu vaux, il/elle vaut, nous valons, vous valez, ils/elles valent

2. *PRESENT SUBJUNCTIVE* je vaille, tu vailles, il/elle vaille, nous valions, vous valiez, ils/elles valent

3. *IMPERFECT* je valais, tu valais, il/elle valait, nous valions, vous valiez, ils/elles valaient

4. *PAST HISTORIC* je valus, tu valus, il/elle valut, nous valûmes, vous valûtes, ils/elles valurent

5. *FUTURE* je vaudrai, tu vaudras, il/elle vaudra, nous vaudrons, vous vaudrez, ils/elles vaudront

6. *CONDITIONAL* je vaudrais, tu vaudrais, il/elle vaudrait, nous vaudrions, vous vaudriez, ils/elles vaudraient

7. *PAST PARTICIPLE* valu

8. *PRESENT PARTICIPLE* valant

70 IRREGULAR VERBS

venir (*to come*) auxiliary 'être': je suis venu *etc*
1. *PRESENT* je viens, tu viens, il/elle vient, nous venons, vous venez, ils/elles viennent
2. *PRESENT SUBJUNCTIVE* je vienne, tu viennes, il/elle vienne, nous venions, vous veniez, ils/elles viennent
3. *IMPERFECT* je venais, tu venais, il/elle venait, nous venions, vous veniez, ils/elles venaient
4. *PAST HISTORIC* je vins, tu vins, il/elle vint, nous vînmes, vous vîntes, ils/elles vinrent
5. *FUTURE* je viendrai, tu viendras, il/elle viendra, nous viendrons, vous viendrez, ils/elles viendront
6. *CONDITIONAL* je viendrais, tu viendrais, il/elle viendrait, nous viendrions, vous viendriez, ils/elles viendraient
7. *PAST PARTICIPLE* venu
8. *PRESENT PARTICIPLE* venant

vêtir (*to dress*) auxiliary 'avoir': j'ai vêtu *etc*
1. *PRESENT* je vêts, tu vêts, il/elle vêt, nous vêtons, vous vêtez, ils/elles vêtent
2. *PRESENT SUBJUNCTIVE* je vête, tu vêtes, il/elle vête, nous vêtions, vous vêtiez, ils/elles vêtent
3. *IMPERFECT* je vêtais, tu vêtais, il/elle vêtait, nous vêtions, vous vêtiez, ils/elles vêtaient
4. *PAST HISTORIC* je vêtis, tu vêtis, il/elle vêtit, nous vêtîmes, vous vêtîtes, ils/elles vêtirent
5. *FUTURE* je vêtirai, tu vêtiras, il/elle vêtira, nous vêtirons, vous vêtirez, ils/elles vêtiront
6. *CONDITIONAL* je vêtirais, tu vêtirais, il/elle vêtirait, nous vêtirions, vous vêtiriez, ils/elles vêtiraient
7. *PAST PARTICIPLE* vêtu
8. *PRESENT PARTICIPLE* vêtant

vivre (*to live*) auxiliary 'avoir': j'ai vécu *etc*
1. *PRESENT* je vis, tu vis, il/elle vit, nous vivons, vous vivez, ils/elles vivent
2. *PRESENT SUBJUNCTIVE* je vive, tu vives, il/elle vive, nous vivions, vous viviez, ils/elles vivent
3. *IMPERFECT* je vivais, tu vivais, il/elle vivait, nous vivions, vous viviez, ils/elles vivaient

IRREGULAR VERBS

4. *PAST HISTORIC* je vécus, tu vécus, il/elle vécut, nous vécûmes, vous vécûtes, ils/elles vécurent
5. *FUTURE* je vivrai, tu vivras, il/elle vivra, nous vivrons, vous vivrez, ils/elles vivront
6. *CONDITIONAL* je vivrais, tu vivrais, il/elle vivrait, nous vivrions, vous vivriez, ils/elles vivraient
7. *PAST PARTICIPLE* vécu
8. *PRESENT PARTICIPLE* vivant

voir (*to see*) auxiliary 'avoir': j'ai vu *etc*
1. *PRESENT* je vois, tu vois, il/elle voit, nous voyons, vous voyez, ils/elles voient
2. *PRESENT SUBJUNCTIVE* je voie, tu voies, il/elle voie, nous voyions, vous voyiez, ils/elles voient
3. *IMPERFECT* je voyais, tu voyais, il/elle voyait, nous voyions, vous voyiez, ils/elles voyaient
4. *PAST HISTORIC* je vis, tu vis, il/elle vit, nous vîmes, vous vîtes, ils/elles virent
5. *FUTURE* je verrai, tu verras, il/elle verra, nous verrons, vous verrez, ils/elles verront
6. *CONDITIONAL* je verrais, tu verrais, il/elle verrait, nous verrions, vous verriez, ils/elles verraient
7. *PAST PARTICIPLE* vu
8. *PRESENT PARTICIPLE* voyant

vouloir (*to want*) auxiliary 'avoir': j'ai voulu *etc*
1. *PRESENT* je veux, tu veux, il/elle veut, nous voulons, vous voulez, ils/elles veulent
2. *PRESENT SUBJUNCTIVE* je veuille, tu veuilles, il/elle veuille, nous voulions, vous vouliez, ils/elles veuillent
3. *IMPERFECT* je voulais, tu voulais, il/elle voulait, nous voulions, vous vouliez, ils/elles voulaient
4. *PAST HISTORIC* je voulus, tu voulus, il/elle voulut, nous voulûmes, vous voulûtes, ils/elles voulurent
5. *FUTURE* je voudrai, tu voudras, il/elle voudra, nous voudrons, vous voudrez, ils/elles voudront
6. *CONDITIONAL* je voudrais, tu voudrais, il/elle voudrait, nous voudrions, vous voudriez, ils voudraient
7. *PAST PARTICIPLE* voulu
8. *PRESENT PARTICIPLE* voulant

LAISSER

laisser 1. (*to leave*) **je vous laisse mon parapluie** *I'll leave you my umbrella;* **laissez-moi votre adresse** *leave me your address*

2. (*in combination with another verb: to let*) **laisser bouillir l'eau pendant cinq minutes** *let the water boil for five minutes;* **il l'a laissé tomber** *he dropped it*

3. **se laisser: se laisser persuader** *to let oneself be persuaded;* **il s'est laissé influencer** *he allowed himself to be swayed*

le, la, les SEE ARTICLES

lequel, laquelle *etc* SEE QUESTIONS

leur, leurs SEE POSSESSIVES

manquer 1. (*to miss*) **je vais manquer le train/le dernier autobus** *I'm going to miss the train/the last bus*

2. **manquer de** (*to lack*): **nous manquons de pain** *we're short of bread*

3. (*to be absent/missing*) **deux élèves manquent** *two pupils are absent;* **il manque deux pages** *there are two pages missing; we're two pages short*

4. **vous me manquez beaucoup** *I miss you a lot*

5. **ne pas manquer de . . .**: **ne manquez pas de me dire** *don't forget to tell me, be sure and tell me*

6. (*nearly . . .*) **j'ai manqué (de) me faire écraser** *I nearly got run over*

ma, mes SEE POSSESSIVES

masculine SEE ADJECTIVES, GENDER

mettre for conjugation see IRREGULAR VERBS

1. (*to put*) **mettez vos livres sur la table** *put your books on the table*

2. (*to put on*) **mets ton manteau, il fait froid** *put your coat on, it's cold*

3. (*to take: time*) **il a mis un an pour le terminer** *it took him a year to finish it*

4. **se mettre: se mettre au travail** *to set to work;* **se**

mettre à lire *to start reading;* **se mettre en colère** *to get angry*

mien, mienne see POSSESSIVES

mieux 1. (*better*) **nous travaillerons mieux demain** *we'll work better tomorrow;* **elle chante mieux que lui** *she sings better than he does;* **se sentir mieux** *to feel better*

2. **faire mieux: il ferait mieux de se taire** *he'd be better to say nothing*

3. **valoir mieux: il vaut mieux s'excuser** *it's better to apologize*

4. **le mieux: la robe qui lui allait le mieux** *the dress which suited her best;* **le mieux serait de les inviter** *the best thing would be to invite them*

5. **de mon mieux** etc: **je l'aide de mon mieux** *I help him as best I can, I do my best to help him;* **faites de votre mieux!** *do your best!*

moins 1. (*less*) **buvez moins, vous vous sentirez mieux** *drink less and you'll feel better;* **elle a moins travaillé cette année** *she has done less work this year;* **je lis moins que toi** *I read less than you do*

2. **moins ... que: elle est moins grande que son frère** *she's smaller than her brother, she's not as tall as her brother;* **c'est moins cher que chez nous** *it's less expensive than at home;* **j'ai moins d'argent que lui** *I have less money than he has*

3. **moins de ...: nous avons eu moins de visiteurs** *we've had fewer visitors, we haven't had so many visitors;* **j'ai moins d'argent que lui** *I have less money than he has;* **cela coûtera moins de 100 francs** *it will cost less than 100 francs*
Note: 'moins d'argent *que* lui', but 'moins *de* 100 francs'

4. (*minus, less*) **6 moins 4 font 2** *6 minus 4 equals 2;* **6 heures moins dix** *ten to 6;* **il est moins cinq** *it's five to;* see also TIME

5. see COMPARATIVE

6. **au moins** *at least*

7. **de moins en moins** *less and less*

mon see POSSESSIVES

negatives

Negative expressions can be split into two groups, depending on constructions:

A	B
ne ... pas *not*	ne ... personne *nobody*
ne ... plus *no longer*	ne ... que *only*
ne ... jamais *never*	ne ... nulle part *nowhere*
ne ... rien *nothing*	ne ... ni ... ni *neither ... nor*

Points to note:
1. Before a vowel **ne** becomes **n'**
2. For the present, imperfect, past historic, future, conditional and imperative, the order is:

   ne + verb + **pas/plus** etc.

   je **ne** fume **pas** *I don't smoke*
   il **n'**est **pas** là *he isn't there*
   elle **ne** voyait **personne** *she didn't see anybody*

   ne dis **rien** *don't say anything*
   n'écoutez **personne** *don't listen to anybody*

   If the verb has an object pronoun, or is inverted (i.e. in questions), the 'ne' comes before the object pronoun:

   ne + object pronoun + verb + **pas/plus** etc.

   je **ne** les aimais **pas** *I didn't like them*
   ne le lui donne **pas** *don't give it to him/her*
   ne vous levez **pas** *don't get up*
   ne l'invitez-vous **pas**? *aren't you inviting him/her?*

3. For the perfect, pluperfect, future perfect and conditional perfect tenses, the order is:

   A **ne ... pas/plus/jamais/rien**:
   ne + auxiliary + **pas/plus** etc + past participle

   je **ne** suis **pas** revenu *I didn't come back*
   il **n'**avait **rien** dit *he hadn't said anything*

   B **ne ... personne/que/nulle part/ni**:
   ne + auxiliary + past participle + **personne/que** etc.

   il **n'**a trouvé **personne** *he didn't find anybody*
   elles **n'**étaient allées **nulle part** *they hadn't gone anywhere*

NEGATIVES

If the verb has an object pronoun, or is inverted, the 'ne' + 'pas' etc occupy the same positions as described above:

A il **ne** l'a **pas** aimé *he didn't like it*
elle **ne** le lui a **pas** donné *she didn't give it to him/her*
ne l'a-t-il **pas** aimé? *didn't he like it?*

B je **ne** l'ai trouvé **nulle part** *I didn't find it anywhere*
n'a-t-il rencontré **personne**? *didn't he meet anybody?*

4. With infinitives the order is:

A **ne pas/plus** etc + infinitive

il préfère **ne pas** parler	*he prefers not to speak*
il a décidé de **ne plus** travailler	*he has decided not to work any longer*
il prétend **ne pas** avoir entendu*	*he claims he hasn't heard*

B **ne** + infinitive + **personne/nulle part** etc

il a prétendu **n**'avoir vu **personne**	*he claimed he didn't see anybody*
elle l'accuse de **ne** s'intéresser à **personne**	*she accuses him of taking no interest in anybody*

*With perfect infinitive, also:
il prétend **n**'avoir **pas** entendu
elle l'accuse de **ne** l'avoir **pas** fait

5. You can begin a sentence with 'rien', 'personne':

rien ne change *nothing changes*
personne n'est venu *nobody came*

6. The following negative expressions can be used on their own:

qui avez-vous vu? **personne**
who did you see? nobody
qu'est-ce qu'il a dit? **rien**
what did he say? nothing
où allez-vous? **nulle part**
where are you going? nowhere
l'avez-vous fait? **pas encore**
have you done it? not yet

est-ce que ça vous dérange? **pas du tout**
do you mind?   not at all

7. Negative words in combination:

je ne la verrai **plus jamais**	*I will never see her again*
elle n'invite **plus personne**	*she no longer invites anybody*
elle n'a **jamais rien** dit	*she has never said anything*
il ne vaut **plus rien**	*it is no longer worth anything*
je ne bois **jamais que** de l'eau	*I only ever drink water*

Note: 'ne ... pas' cannot be combined with 'jamais', 'plus' etc.

nos, notre *etc* see POSSESSIVES

numbers

CARDINAL	ORDINAL
1 un (une)	1st premier (première) 1er (1ère)
2 deux	2nd deuxième 2e, 2ème
3 trois	3rd troisième 3e, 3ème
4 quatre	4th quatrième
5 cinq	5th cinquième
6 six	6th sixième
7 sept	7th septième
8 huit	8th huitième
9 neuf	9th neuvième
10 dix	10th dixième
11 onze	11th onzième
12 douze	12th douzième
13 treize	13th treizième
14 quatorze	14th quatorzième
15 quinze	15th quinzième
16 seize	16th seizième
17 dix-sept	17th dix-septième
18 dix-huit	18th dix-huitième
19 dix-neuf	19th dix-neuvième
20 vingt	20th vingtième
21 vingt et un (une)	21st vingt et unième
22 vingt-deux	22nd vingt-deuxième

	CARDINAL		*ORDINAL*
30	trente	**30th**	trentième
31	trente et un (une)		*etc*
40	quarante		
50	cinquante		
60	soixante		
70	soixante-dix		
71	soixante et onze		
72	soixante-douze		
80	quatre-vingts		
90	quatre-vingt-dix		
91	quatre-vingt-onze		
100	cent	**100th**	centième
101	cent un (une)	**101st**	cent unième
200	deux cents		*etc*
250	deux cent cinquante		
1000	mille		
1001	mille un (une)		
2,000	deux mille, 2 000		
1,000,000	un million, 1 000 000 *or* 1.000.000		
2,000,000	deux millions, 2 000 000 *or* 2.000.000		

Notes

Cardinal numbers

(a) Used as adjectives, these numbers come before the noun: trois enfants *three children*
deux cents spectateurs
two hundred spectators

'Une' – the feminine form of 'un' – must be used when the noun is feminine:

trente et une demandes *thirty one applications*
'Million' is always followed by 'de' before the noun:

un million de francs *a million francs*; cinq millions d'abonnés *five million subscribers*

(b) With the exception of 'un (une)' (see note (e)), these numbers are used for dates:
le cinq mars *the fifth of March*

(c) For telephone numbers see below.

(d) Note the use of 'millier':
un millier de véhicules *(about) a thousand vehicles*

NUMBERS 77

il y en avait des milliers *there were thousands of them*

(e) In French the comma is used as a decimal point and the full-stop (or a space) is used for thousands (as illustrated above):
0,2 zéro virgule deux
3,86 trois virgule quatre-vingt six

Ordinal numbers
(a) Used as adjectives, these numbers come before the noun:
au quatrième étage *on the fourth floor*
le vingtième siècle *the twentieth century*
(b) French uses 'premier' for the first day of the month: le premier mai *the first of May*
(c) 'Second' (feminine: 'seconde') is an alternative to 'deuxième'

◆ *APPROXIMATE NUMBERS*
French indicates that a number is approximate by adding '-aine' (note the changes to spelling):
une dizaine *about ten*; une vingtaine *about twenty*; une trentaine *about thirty*; une cinquantaine *about fifty*.
Thus: une dizaine de chemises *about ten shirts*; une quarantaine d'années *about forty years*

Alternatively, 'environ' (*about*) can be used:
il y en avait environ dix *there were about ten of them*

◆ *FRACTIONS*
$\frac{1}{4}$	un quart
$\frac{1}{2}$	un demi, une demie
$\frac{3}{4}$	trois quarts
$\frac{1}{3}$	un tiers
$\frac{2}{3}$	deux tiers
$\frac{1}{5}$	un cinquième
$\frac{1}{8}$	un huitième
$\frac{1}{12}$	un douzième
$\frac{1}{20}$	un vingtième

Thus: un kilo et demi *1½ kilos*
deux heures et demie *2½ hours*
les trois quarts du terrain *¾ of the land*

♦ DIMENSIONS
Note the following constructions:
avoir 30 cm. de longueur/de largeur/de hauteur or **être long/large/haut de 30 cm.**
to be 30 cm long/broad/high
ma chambre a 4 mètres de long sur 3 de large
my bedroom is 4 metres long by 3 metres wide

♦ DISTANCE
combien y a-t-il d'ici jusqu'à Rouen? il y a 20 km
how far is it (from here) to Rouen? it's 20 km
à quelle distance est l'aéroport? Il est à 7 km (de distance)
how far (away) is the airport? It's 7 km.

♦ TELEPHONE NUMBERS
These are read out as blocks of two- or three-figure numbers:
230810 = 23/08/10 = vingt-trois/zéro huit/dix
2305145 = 230/51/45 = deux cent trente/cinquante et un/quarante-cinq

on 1. *(impersonal)* **on peut y ajouter du sucre** *you (or we) can add sugar to it*

2. *(we)* **on en parlera plus tard** *we'll talk about it later*

3. *(somebody)* **on vous demande au téléphone** *there's somebody on the phone for you, you're wanted on the phone*

4. *(people)* **que va-t-on penser?** *what will people think?*

Note that 'on' with an active verb form is often used where the PASSIVE would be used in English: **on peut le réparer facilement** *it is easily repaired;* **on nous a dit qu'il était malade** *we were told he was ill;* **on m'a donné ce livre** *I was given this book*

où 1. *(question)* **où allez-vous?** *where are you going?;* **d'où venez-vous?** *where do you come from?; where are you coming from?*

2. *(as a pronoun: place or time)* **le jour où il reviendra** *the day he comes back;* **l'endroit où tu l'as mis** *the place where you put it*

par 1. (*direction*) **passez par le jardin** *go through the garden;* **passer par Paris/la France** *to go via Paris/France;* **entrez par la porte de droite** *go in the right-hand door;* **regarder par la fenêtre** *to look out of the window*

2. (*per*) **plusieurs fois par jour** *several times a/per day;* **je gagne 5000 francs par mois** *I earn 5000 francs a month*

3. (*agent, means*) **il a été renversé par une voiture** *he was knocked down by a car;* **j'ai appris la nouvelle par mon frère** *I learned the news from my brother;* **par la poste** *by post, through the post*

pas see NEGATIVES

passer 1. (*to give*) **passe-moi un crayon** *pass me a pencil;* **il m'a passé un livre** *he handed me a book*

2. **passer un examen** *to sit an exam*

3. (*to call (in)*) **nous passerons dans la soirée** *we'll call in the evening;* **nous passerons prendre nos affaires** *we'll call for our things, we'll pick up our things*

4. **se passer: ça s'est passé le mois dernier** *it happened last month;* **ça s'est bien passé** *it went well*

5. **se passer de: il s'est passé de mon aide** *he did without my help*

passive

Just as English forms the passive with tenses of 'to be'+past participle, French forms the passive with tenses of 'être'+past participle:

    j'ai été puni(e) par le professeur *I was punished by the teacher*

    elle sera punie *she will be punished*

    nous avons été puni(e)s *we have been punished*

The past participle must 'agree' with the subject:
- adding 'e' if the subject is feminine singular
- adding 's' if the subject is masculine plural
- adding 'es' if the subject is feminine plural

The passive is used less often in French than in English. For an alternative to the passive form see ON, REFLEXIVE VERBS

personal pronouns

♦ TABLE OF PERSONAL PRONOUNS

	1	2	3	4	5
		OBJECT			EMPHATIC
	SUBJECT			REFLEXIVE	with
		DIRECT	INDIRECT		PREPOSITION
	je, j'	me, m'	me, m'	me, m'	moi
	I	*me*	*(to) me*	*myself*	*me*
	tu	te, t'	te, t'	te, t'	toi
	you	*you*	*(to) you*	*yourself*	*you*
	il	le, l'	lui	se, s'	lui
	he/it	*him/it*	*(to) him/it*	*himself/itself*	*him/it*
	elle	la, l'	lui	se, s'	elle
	she/it	*her/it*	*(to) her/it*	*herself/itself*	*her/it*
	on			se	soi
	one			*oneself*	*oneself*
	nous	nous	nous	nous	nous
	we	*us*	*(to) us*	*ourselves*	*us*
	vous	vous	vous	vous	vous
	you	*you*	*(to) you*	*yourself; yourselves*	*you*
	ils	les	leur	se, s'	eux
	they	*them*	*(to) them*	*themselves*	*them*
	elles	les	leur	se, s'	elles
	they	*them*	*(to) them*	*themselves*	*them*

♦ SUBJECT PRONOUNS

1. **je** > **j'** before a vowel, an h mute, Y or EN:
   j'ai faim; j'y vais etc.
   Note however: puis-je entrer/avoir...? *may I come in/have...?*
2. '**tu**' versus '**vous**':
   You should use '**tu**' – the familiar form of 'you' singular – when addressing a relative, a child, a friend, or someone you know very well; you should use '**vous**' – the formal or polite form of 'you' singular *or* plural – in other cases.
3. '**il**' (*he/it*) replaces a masculine singular noun
   '**elle**' (*she/it*) replaces a feminine singular noun

'ils' (*they*) replaces a masculine plural noun
'elles' (*they*) replaces a feminine plural noun:

quel âge a ton frère? – **il** a dix ans
how old is your brother? – he's ten
as-tu vu mon parapluie? – **il** est dans le hall
have you seen my umbrella? – it's in the hall
as-tu vu ma serviette: **elle** était sur la table?
have you seen my briefcase? it was on the table
quand **ils** étaient plus jeunes, mes parents ...
when they were younger, my parents ...

See also CE

Note: **'il'** is used in expressions relating to the weather and to time:

il fait froid/il fait du brouillard *it's cold/foggy*
il est sept heures et demie *it's half past seven*

♦ *OBJECT PRONOUNS, REFLEXIVE PRONOUNS*

1. **me, te, se > m', t', s'** before a vowel, an h mute, Y or EN:

    il **m'**aime — *he loves me*
    elle **t'**en a donné deux — *she gave you two*

2. In positive commands **me** and **te** become **moi** and **toi**:

    aidez-**moi** — *help me*
    donne-**moi** la main — *give me your hand*

3. Direct versus indirect:
   With the exception of **'le', 'la', 'l'', 'les', 'lui'** and **'leur'**, (i.e. 3rd person pronouns), direct and indirect object pronouns in French have the same form:

    il **me** connaît — *he knows me*
    il **me** parle — *he talks to me*
    elle **nous** aime — *she likes us*
    elle **nous** écrit — *she writes to us*

♦ **le, la, l', les**: direct object pronouns

le, la become **l'** before a vowel, an h mute, Y or EN:
je **l'**ai vu *I saw him/it*
Note however: faites-**le** entrer *show him in*

le, l' (*him/it*) replaces a masculine singular noun
la, l' (*her/it*) replaces a feminine singular noun
les (*them*) replaces a masculine or feminine plural noun:

mon appareil-photo ne marche pas: pouvez-vous **le** réparer?
my camera isn't working — can you repair it?
j'ai deux voisins mais je ne **les** vois pas souvent
I have two neighbours, but I don't often see them

◆ **lui, leur**: indirect object pronouns

lui = *(to) him/her/it*   **leur** = *(to) them*

Compare:
je le/la connais	*I know him/her*
je **lui** écris	*I write to him/her*
nous l'aimons	*we like him/her*
nous **lui** envoyons des lettres	*we send him/her letters*
tu les as choisis	*you chose them*
tu **leur** as donné l'argent	*you gave them the money*

Note: You can tell from a French construction whether the verb takes a direct object, an indirect object or both:

e.g. demander quelque chose (*direct*)
to ask for something
demander quelque chose (*direct*) à quelqu'un (*indirect*)
to ask somebody for something
demander à quelqu'un (*indirect*) de faire quelque chose
to ask somebody to do something

4. Reflexive verbs and their pronouns are dealt with at REFLEXIVE VERBS.
Note however that '**te**' becomes '**toi**' in positive commands:

couche-**toi**! *go to bed!*
lève-**toi**! *stand up!*
but: ne **t'**assieds pas! *don't sit down!*
ne **te** lève pas! *don't stand up!*

PERSONAL PRONOUNS

♦ EMPHATIC PRONOUNS

1. The emphatic form of the pronoun is used:
   a. for emphasis:
      toi, tu peux y aller, mais **moi**, je reste ici
      YOU can go, but I'M staying here
   b. when the pronoun is used on its own:
      qui est-ce? – **moi** *who is it? – me*
   c. when you have double subjects of the type 'you and I', 'she and her mother':
      lui et son fils vont à la pêche
      he and his son go fishing
      vous et **moi** pouvons le faire
      you and I can do it
   d. in comparative constructions:
      plus âgé que **moi** *older than me*
   e. after 'c'est, ce sont' etc:
      c'est **lui** *it's him*
      ce sont **eux** *it's them*
   f. after 'ne ... que':
      elles ne détestent que **lui** *they only hate him*
   g. with '-même(s)' for greater emphasis:
      moi-même *myself*
      toi-même *yourself*
      lui-même *himself/itself*
      elle-même *herself/itself*
      soi-même *oneself*
      nous-mêmes *ourselves*
      vous-même(s) *yourself(yourselves)*
      eux-mêmes *themselves*
      elles-mêmes *themselves*
      je l'ai fait **moi-même** *I did it myself*
   h. after a preposition:
      quant à **moi** *as for me*
      chez **eux** *at their house*
      sans **elle** *without her*
      elle se fie à **lui** *she trusts him*
      nous pensons à **vous** *we are thinking about you*

2. The emphatic pronoun is only used for people or animals, not things:

j'aime bien travailler avec **lui** *I like working with him (e.g. a friend)*

j'aime mieux travailler avec **celui-ci** *I prefer working with this one (e.g. a dictionary)*

3. For uses of **soi** see SOI

◆ *POSITION OF OBJECT PRONOUNS*

1. All object pronouns shown in columns 2 – 4 of the Table come before the verb or its auxiliary in a sentence:

je **la** vois	*I see her*
je **l'**ai vue	*I saw her*
il **lui** écrit	*he writes to him/her*
il **lui** avait écrit	*he had written to him/her*
elle **se** lève	*she gets up*
elle **s'**est levée	*she got up*
nous ne **les** aimons pas	*we don't like them*
où est-ce que vous **les** avez laissés?	*where did you leave them?*
ne **l'**aimez-vous pas?	*don't you like him/her/it?*

2. In positive commands (e.g. 'take it', 'go away') the pronoun comes *after* the verb and is joined to it by a hyphen:

prenez-**le** *take it*
allez-**vous**-en *go away*
regarde-**nous** *look at us*

Note: '**me**' and '**te**' become '**moi**' and '**toi**' *except before* Y *or* EN:

aidez-**moi** *help me*
tais-**toi** *be quiet*
but:
donnez-**m'**en *give me some*

3. The object pronoun of an infinitive following a verb usually comes before the infinitive:

je vais **l'**aider *I'm going to help him/her*
il veut **nous** voir *he wants to see us*

86 PERSONNE

♦ *ORDER OF OBJECT PRONOUNS*
Where more than one object pronoun accompanies the verb the order is as follows:

1. Before the verb:

me
te
se   *before*   le / la / les   *before*   lui / leur   *before* y *before* en
nous
vous

   il **me les** décrit   *he describes them to me*
   je **le lui** explique   *I explain it to him/her*
   il **s'en** est souvenu   *he remembered it*

2. After the verb: *direct* before *indirect:*

le / la / les   *before*   moi (m') / toi (t') / lui / nous / vous / leur   *before* y   *before* en

   donnez-**le-moi**   *give it to me*
   donnez-**m'en**   *give me some*
   expliquez-**le-nous**   *explain it to us*

personne 1. **personne n'est venu** *nobody came;* **nous n'inviterons personne** *we won't invite anybody;* **il n'y a personne à la maison** *there's nobody in*

2. **qui t'a vu? — personne** *who saw you? — nobody;* **qui as-tu vu? — personne** *who did you see? — nobody;* **qui le sait? — presque personne** *who knows about it? — hardly anyone*

3. **sans que personne nous voie** *without anybody seeing us;* **je le sais mieux que personne** *I know better than anybody;* note the use of the SUBJUNCTIVE after 'sans que personne ...'

peu 1. **il fume peu** *he doesn't smoke much;* **il gagne peu** *he doesn't earn very much;* **il travaille trop peu** *he doesn't work enough*

2. **peu de...**: **nous avons peu de temps** *we don't*

have much time; **il a peu d'amis** *he hasn't many friends, he has few friends*

3. **un peu plus/moins de pain** *a little more/less bread;* **un peu plus/moins de spectateurs** *slightly more/fewer spectators*

4. **peu à peu** *little by little, gradually*

5. **à peu près** *just about, almost;* **à peu près cinq minutes** *about five minutes*

6. **peu avant** *shortly before;* **c'est peu intéressant** *it's not very interesting*

plurals

PLURALS OF NOUNS

1. General rule: **singular + s**:

   le garçon   les garçons
   la fille   les filles

2. 'Semi-irregular' plurals:

SINGULAR ENDING	PLURAL ENDING	EXAMPLE		
-s, -x, -z	no change	le bas les bas	la voix les voix	le nez les nez
-au, -eau	-x	le tuyau les tuyaux	le bateau les bateaux	
-eu*	-x	le feu les feux		
-al*	-aux	le journal les journaux	le cheval les chevaux	
-ail	-aux	le travail les travaux	le vitrail les vitraux	

* Common exceptions:
  le pneu, les pneus
  le bal, les bals
  le festival, les festivals

3. Most words ending in **-ou** form their plural regularly by adding **-s**, but there are some which add **-x**. The most common of these are:

   le bijou, le caillou, le chou, le genou, le hibou, le joujou, le pou.

4. Common irregular plurals:
l'œil > les yeux
le monsieur > les messieurs
Madame > Mesdames
Mademoiselle > Mesdemoiselles

5. Compound nouns (chauve-souris, chemin de fer, garde-malade etc): these follow fairly complex rules for the formation of the plural. It is best to consult a dictionary

See also GENDER, ADJECTIVES

plus
1. ne ... plus: nous n'irons plus au cinéma *we won't go to the cinema any more;* **il n'en a plus** *he hasn't got any left;* **il n'y en a plus** *there isn't any left;* **il n'en a plus besoin** *he doesn't need it any longer;* **il n'y a plus de beurre** *there's no more butter;* see also NEGATIVES

2. plus ... que: Paul est plus grand que son cousin *Paul is taller than his cousin;* **il en a plus que moi** *he has more than me*

3. plus de ...: je veux plus d'argent *I want more money;* **il a plus de livres que de disques** *he has more books than records;* **elle a plus de chance que son frère** *she is luckier than her brother;* **plus de dix personnes m'ont parlé** *more than ten people spoke to me*

Note 'plus de chance *que* moi', but 'plus *de* dix personnes'; see also COMPARATIVE

4. en plus: elle a travaillé trois heures en plus *she worked three hours extra;* **elle est revenue avec deux clients en plus** *she came back with two extra clients;* **en plus de cela, il a perdu l'adresse** *on top of that, he lost the address*

5. plus ... plus/moins: plus on travaille, moins on s'ennuie *the more you work, the less you get bored;* **plus il arrivait de monde, plus il s'inquiétait** *the more people arrived, the more concerned he became*

plusieurs
1. il y a plusieurs solutions *there are several solutions;* **je l'ai appelé plusieurs fois** *I called him several times*

2. ils/elles sont plusieurs *there are several of them;* **nous en avons cassé plusieurs** *we've broken several (of them);* note the use of the same form, whether for the masculine or the feminine

possessives

♦ **mon, ma, mes** etc — *my* etc: the possessive adjective

Note that the form of the possessive adjective depends on the gender of the noun, and on whether it is singular or plural:

SINGULAR NOUN

MASCULINE		FEMININE		
mon*	vélo	ma	vie	*my* ...
ton*	père	ta	mère	*your* ...
son*	avis	sa	fin	*his/her/its* ...
notre	but	notre	aide	*our* ...
votre	emploi	votre	fille	*your* ...
leur	patron	leur	chambre	*their* ...

PLURAL NOUN

MASCULINE/FEMININE

mes	frères/sœurs	*my* ...
tes	espoirs/idées	*your* ...
ses	frais/raisons	*his/her/its* ...
nos	amis/amies	*our* ...
vos	conseils/autos	*your* ...
leurs	noms/voix	*their* ...

* The asterisked forms are also used with a feminine noun beginning with a vowel or h mute:
  mon école
  ton histoire
  son attitude

Points to note:

1. Whether the possessor is male or female does not affect the form of the possessive adjective; what matters is the gender of the noun:

   elle m'a prêté **son** vélo/**sa** voiture
   she lent me her bike/car
   il m'a prêté **son** vélo/**sa** voiture
   he lent me his bike/car

90 POSSESSIVES

2. 'ton, ta, tes' are used when speaking to a person addressed as 'tu'; 'votre, vos' are used when speaking to a person/persons addressed as 'vous' (see PERSONAL PRONOUNS)

3. 'son, sa, ses' also translate 'one's':
   aimer sa patrie   *to love one's country*

♦ **le mien, le tien** etc — mine etc: the possessive pronoun

Voici mon billet. Où est **le tien/le vôtre**?
Here is my ticket. Where is yours? (= your ticket)
Vous n'avez pas de montre? Empruntez **la mienne**.
Don't you have a watch? Borrow mine (= my watch)

A possessive pronoun (yours, mine etc) replaces a noun already referred to (ticket, watch etc). In French, the form of the possessive pronoun depends on whether the noun is masculine or feminine, singular or plural:

SINGULAR NOUN		PLURAL NOUN		
MASCULINE	FEMININE	MASCULINE	FEMININE	
le mien	la mienne	les miens	les miennes	*mine*
le tien	la tienne	les tiens	les tiennes	*yours*
le sien	la sienne	les siens	les siennes	*his/hers*
le nôtre	la nôtre	les nôtres	les nôtres	*ours*
le vôtre	la vôtre	les vôtres	les vôtres	*yours*
le leur	la leur	les leurs	les leurs	*theirs*

Points to note:

1. It does not matter whether the possessor is male or female:

   prenez { le sien / la sienne / les siens / les siennes }   *take his/hers*

2. 'le tien', 'la tienne' etc are used when speaking to a person addressed as 'tu'; 'le vôtre', 'la vôtre' etc are used when speaking to a person/persons addressed as 'vous' (see PERSONAL PRONOUNS)

3. 'le sien', 'la sienne' etc also translate 'one's own':
   quelquefois on préfère la cuisine des autres à **la**

sienne *sometimes one prefers other people's cooking to one's own*

4. Note that after 'à' and 'de' the definite articles 'le' and 'les' contract:

e.g. je préfère ton dessin **au** leur
I prefer your drawing to theirs
la rencontre de mes parents et **des** vôtres
the meeting of my parents and yours

pour 1. (*for*) **ces fleurs sont pour toi** *these flowers are for you;* **ce n'est pas un livre pour enfants** *it's not a book for children*

2. (*direction*) **je pars pour Rome à midi** *I leave for Rome at noon*

3. (*in order to*) **je l'ai fait pour vous aider** *I did it to help you;* **j'en ai assez pour lui prêter 50 francs** *I've enough to lend him 50 francs*

4. **pour que: pour que nous sachions** *so that we know;* note the use of the SUBJUNCTIVE

5. (*quantity*) **donnez-moi pour 30 francs d'essence** *give me 30 francs' worth of petrol.*

pouvoir for conjugation see IRREGULAR VERBS

1. (*ability*) **pouvoir faire quelque chose** *to be able to do something;* **il peut le faire facilement** *he can easily do it;* **il pourra marcher avec des béquilles** *he'll be able to get about on crutches*

2. (*permission*) **tu peux y aller** *you can go;* **puis-je me servir de vin?** *may I help myself to some wine?*

3. (*possibility*) **il se pourrait qu'il pleuve** *it might well rain;* **il se peut qu'il n'ait pas reçu ta lettre** *he may not have received your letter;* note the use of the SUBJUNCTIVE

4. (*expressing a wish*) **il aurait pu venir!** *he might have come!, he could have come!;* **il pourrait se dépêcher!** *he could hurry up a bit!*

5. **je n'en peux plus!** *I'm exhausted!; I can't take any more!*

prepositions see A, APRÈS, AVANT, DANS, DE, DEPUIS, EN, PAR, POUR, SANS

prepositional constructions

The following constructions illustrate the different uses of the prepositions **de** and **à**, with particular reference to the various ways they are translated in English. 'Faire' (*to do*) represents the infinitive and 'qch' (an abbreviation of 'quelque chose' (*something*)) and 'qn' (an abbreviation of 'quelqu'un' (*somebody*)) represent the thing or person concerned.

1. adjective+de+infinitive
   capable de faire *able to do; capable of doing*
   content de faire *happy to do*
   heureux de faire *happy to do*
   impatient de faire *impatient/eager to do*

2. adjective+de+noun
   capable de qch *capable of sth*
   enchanté de qch *delighted with sth*
   furieux de qch *furious at sth*
   reconnaissant de qch *grateful for sth*
   responsable de qch *responsible for sth*
   satisfait de qch *satisfied with sth*
   surpris de qch *surprised at sth*

3. adjective+à+noun
   apte à qch *suitable for sth, fit for sth*

4. verb+de
   blâmer qn de qch *to blame sb for sth*
   dépendre de qn/qch *to depend on sb/sth*
   s'étonner de qch *to be surprised at sth*
   s'excuser de qch *to apologize for sth*
   féliciter qn de qch *to congratulate sb on sth*
   jouir de qch *to enjoy sth*
   se moquer de qn/qch *to make fun of sb/sth*
   parler de qch/qn *to talk about sth/sb*
   se passer de qch *to do without sth*
   rire de qn/qch *to laugh at sb/sth*
   se servir de qch/ qn *to use sth/sb*
   se souvenir de qch/qn *to remember sth/sb*

5. verb+à
   se fier à qn *to trust sb*
   s'habituer à qch *to get used to sth*

nuire à qn *to harm sb*
obéir à qn *to obey sb*
plaire à qn *to please sb*
renoncer à qch *to give sth up*
ressembler à qn/qch *to resemble sb/sth*

apprendre qch à qn *to teach sb sth; to tell sb sth*
défendre qch à qn *to forbid sb sth*
demander qch à qn *to ask sb sth; to ask sb for sth*
dire qch à qn *to tell sb sth*
pardonner qch à qn *to forgive sb for sth*
permettre qch à qn *to allow sb sth*

acheter qch à qn *to buy sth from sb or for sb*
cacher qch à qn *to hide sth from sb*
emprunter qch à qn *to borrow sth from sb*
enlever qch à qn *to take sth (away) from sb*
prendre qch à qn *to take sth from sb*

Note: the following constructions have a preposition in English but not in French:
to wait for sb/sth **attendre qn/qch**
to look for sth/sb **chercher qch/qn**
to listen to sb/sth **écouter qn/qch**
to hope for sth **espérer qch**
to pay for sth **payer qch**
to look at sb/sth **regarder qn/qch**

presque 1. (*almost*) **j'ai presque terminé** *I have nearly finished;* **j'ai lu presque tout le livre** *I've read almost the whole book*

2. (*hardly*) **je n'ai vu presque personne** *I hardly saw anyone;* **il n'a presque rien dit** *he hardly spoke at all;* **ils n'ont presque plus d'argent** *they have hardly any money left.*

pronouns   see DEMONSTRATIVES, EN, PERSONAL PRONOUNS, POSSESSIVES, QUESTIONS, SENTENCES, Y

pronunciation
French pronunciation is often shown by means of symbols from the International Phonetic Alphabet. Most of these symbols are the letters of the alphabet with the same value as their English counterparts;

PRONUNCIATION

the few which have different values or which require explanation are shown in the table below:

IPA	Pronounced	IPA	Pronounced
[ɑ]	ah	[ɛ̃]	$ūñ^3$
[a]	as in 'cat'	[ɑ̃]	$āñ^4$
[e]	ay	[ɔ̃]	$ōñ^5$
[ɛ]	eh	[œ̃]	$ūñ^3$
[i]	ee	[j]	y^6
[ɔ]	as in 'pot'	[w]	w^7
[o]	oh	[ɥ]	w^7
[u]	oo	[ʃ]	sh
[y]	$\overline{oo}^1$	[ʒ]	j^8
[ə]	uh^2	[ʀ]	r^9
[ø]	uh^2	[ɲ]	ny^{10}
[œ]	as in 'bird'	[ŋ]	ng^{11}

1. Round your lips to say *oo*, then try to say *ee*
2. As in *a*bove
3. As in mer*ing*ue
4. As in dé*ten*te
5. As in *bon* voyage
6. As in *y*et
7. As in *w*ell
8. As in mea*s*ure
9. The 'r' is produced with the uvula (try gargling!)
10. As in o*ni*on
11. As in campi*ng*

The symbol ['] (which is applicable to a few words beginning with an 'h') indicates that *le/la, je, me, te* etc do *not* contract to *l', j', m'* etc:

> haie ['ɛ]: la haie; haïr ['aiʀ]: je hais
> but ('h mute or aspirate')
> hélicoptère [elikɔptɛʀ]: l'hélicoptère
> habiter [abite]: j'habite

♦ spelling and pronunciation

Outlined below with their IPA values are those letters or groups of letters whose pronunciation differs from English. Groups of letters shown here never cross syllable boundaries, i.e. aim as in 'faim', not 'ai-mer'; ail as in 'travail', not 'ai-lier'

PRONUNCIATION 95

SPELLING	IPA	SPELLING	IPA
a	[a]/[ɑ]	in, im, în	[ɛ̃]
à	[a]	j	[ʒ]
â	[ɑ]	ll	[l]
ai, aî	[ɛ]/[e]	as in 'travailler'	[j]
-ail(l)	[ɑj]	o	[ɔ]/[ʊ]
-ain, aim	[ɛ̃]	ô	[o]
-an, am	[ɑ̃]	oe	[wa]
au	[o]	oe, oeu	[œ]
ç	[s]	œil(l)	[œj]
c (+e/i)	[s]	oi, oî	[wa]
ch	[ʃ]	oin	[wɛ̃]
d: see note 2		on, om	[ɔ̃]
e	[ɛ]/[e]	ou, oû	[u]
	[ə]	as in 'oui'	[w]
see notes below		où	[u]
é	[e]	ouill	[uj]
è, ê	[ɛ]	qu	[k]
eau	[o]	s: see note 2	
ei	[ɛ]	t: see note 2	
eil(l)	[ɛj]	th	[t]
ein	[ɛ̃]	tion	[sjɔ̃]
en, em	[ɑ̃]	u, û	[y]
-er	[e]	as in 'huile'	[ɥ]
eu, eû	[ø]/[œ]	ueil(l)	[œj]
euil(l)	[œj]	un, um	[œ̃]
-ez	[e]	x: see note 2	
g (+e/i)	[ʒ]	y	[i]
gn	[ɲ]	as in 'yoga'	[j]
h	silent	yn, ym	[ɛ̃]
i, î	[i]		
as in 'vieux'	[j]		

Note: **Noël** [nɔɛl]; **maïs** [mais]

Notes: *how position affects pronunciation*
1. i) A final 'e' is usually silent:
    amie [ami]   blessée [blese]   père [pɛʀ]
    déçue [desy]   triste [tʀist]   quelle [kɛl]

  ii) When an 'e' – the regular feminine ending – follows the nasal groups 'ain', 'in', 'ein' *etc*, the 'n' is sounded and the vowel sound changes. This is also the case for the nasal groups 'on', 'an', 'en' which double the 'n' before adding 'e':

MASCULINE	FEMININE
cousin [kuzẽ]	cousine [kuzin]
vain [vẽ]	vaine [vɛn]
plein [plẽ]	pleine [plɛn]
plan [plã]	plane [plan]
un [œ̃]	une [yn]
bon [bɔ̃]	bonne [bɔn]
italien [italjẽ]	italienne [italjɛn]
paysan [peizã]	paysanne [peizan]

2. i) A final 'd', 's', 't' or 'x' is usually silent:

retard [Rətar]   nid [ni]
bois [bwa]   ses [se]
lit [li]   mets [mɛ]
aux [o]   seaux [so]

a) Adding an 'e' – the regular feminine ending – results in 'd', 's' and 't' being pronounced:

MASCULINE	FEMININE
grand [gRɔ̃]	grande [gRɔ̃d]
gris [gRi]	grise [gRiz]
petit [pəti]	petite [pətit]

b) Adding an 's' – the regular plural ending –, or 'x' – an irregular plural ending – does not alter the pronunciation:

SINGULAR	PLURAL
train [tRẽ]	trains [tRẽ]
ville [vil]	villes [vil]
beau [bo]	beaux [bo]
feu [fø]	feux [fø]

ii) Between words if the next word begins with a vowel or a mute h the 's' or 'x' may be sounded [z] (this is called 'liaison'):
de bons articles [də bɔ̃z aRtiklə]
de beaux hommes [də boz ɔm]
les Etats-Unis [lez etaz yni]
les habitants des Hébrides [lez abitã dez ebRid]

◆ **the alphabet**

a	[a]	j	[ʒi]	s	[ɛs]
b	[be]	k	[ka]	t	[te]
c	[se]	l	[ɛl]	u	[y]
d	[de]	m	[ɛm]	v	[ve]
e	[ə]	n	[ɛn]	w	[dubləvc]
f	[ɛf]	o	[o]	x	[iks]
g	[ʒe]	p	[pe]	y	[igʀɛk]
h	[aʃ]	q	[ky]	z	[zɛd]
i	[i]	r	[ɛʀ]		

que 1. (*interrogative*) **que veux-tu?** *what do you want?*; see also QUESTIONS

2. (*relative*) **le film que j'ai vu** *the film I saw*; see also SENTENCES, VERB FORMS

3. (*than, as*) **il est plus grand que moi** *he's taller than me*; **c'est aussi cher qu'en France** *it's as expensive as in France*

4. (*that*) **je sais qu'il est parti** *I know he has left*; see also CONJUNCTIONS, SENTENCES

5. (*whether*) **que tu viennes ou non** *whether you are coming or not*; note the use of the SUBJUNCTIVE

quelque 1. (*some*) **cela fait quelque temps que je ne l'ai vu** *it's been some time since I saw him*

2. **il y avait quelque 500 personnes** *there were some 500 people*
See also QUELQUES

quelque chose 1. (*something*) **j'ai entendu quelque chose** *I heard something*

2. (*anything*) **avez-vous trouvé quelque chose?** *did you find anything?*

quelquefois *sometimes*

quelque part *somewhere*

quelques: **nous avons quelques chaises en trop** *we have a few extra chairs*; **les quelques fois que nous sommes allés à la campagne** *the few times we went to the country*

quelques-uns, quelques-unes *some, a few*

quelqu'un
1. (*someone*) **quelqu'un m'a dit que...** *someone told me that...*

2. (*anyone*) **as-tu vu quelqu'un?** *did you see anyone?*

questions
♦ *WITHOUT QUESTION WORDS*

A. Inversion

1. If the subject is PERSONAL PRONOUN, or ON (one, you), or CE (it, this):
    order = verb + subject (joined by a hyphen):
    e.g. **venez-vous?** *are you coming?*
    sont-ils arrivés? *have they arrived?*
    est-ce vrai? *is it true?*
    vous **souvenez-vous?** *do you remember?*
    doit-on s'inscrire? *does one have to register?*

If the verb ends in a vowel, a 't' is inserted between the verb and subject:
e.g. **pleure-t-elle?** *is she crying?*
    les **aime-t-il?** *does he like them?*

Note that French and English form a question in the same way, i.e. they invert the normal order of a statement (subject and verb) so that the verb comes first:

STATEMENT	QUESTION
vous venez >	**venez-vous?**
you are coming	*are you coming?*
c'est vrai >	**est-ce vrai?**
it's true	*is it true?*
vous vous souvenez >	**vous souvenez-vous?**
you remember	*do you remember?*

2. If the subject is a noun, or a pronoun *other than* a personal pronoun:
    order = subject + verb + personal pronoun
            (added, and joined to verb by a hyphen)
    e.g. ceux-là **sont-ils** frais? *are those fresh?*
    le train **est-il** parti? *has the train left?*

votre mère **travaille-t-elle** toujours?
does your mother still work?

B. est-ce que...?
order = est-ce que + subject + verb

est-ce que vous venez? *are you coming?*
est-ce que le train est parti? *has the train left?*
est-ce qu'ils sont venus? *have they come?*
est-ce que vous vous êtes bien amusés? *did you enjoy yourselves?*

C. Intonation
In spoken French, you can simply use intonation, raising your voice at the end of the sentence:

e.g. vous ve**nez**? *are you coming?*
il est ma**lade**? *is he ill?*

♦ *WITH QUESTION WORDS*

où: où allez-vous? *where are you going?*
est-ce que vous allez?
où se trouve le cinéma? *where is the cinema?*

quand: quand arrive-t-elle? *when is she arriving?*
est-ce qu'elle arrive?

pourquoi: pourquoi riez-vous? *why are you*
est-ce que vous riez? *laughing?*

comment: comment le savait-il? *how did he know?*
comment allez-vous? *how are you?*

combien: combien ça coûte? *how much does it cost?*
combien y en a-t-il? *how many are there?*

combien de: combien de temps avez-vous?
how much time have you got?
combien d'argent avez-vous?
how much money have you got?

combien de voitures y a-t-il?
how many cars are there?
combien d'enfants y a-t-il?
how many children are there?

...n'est-ce pas?
il fait beau, n'est-ce pas?
the weather's nice, isn't it?

il mentait, n'est-ce pas?
he was lying, wasn't he?
tu reviendras, n'est-ce pas?
you'll come back, won't you?

♦ **qui (est-ce qui/que)** *who?*

qui est là? ⎫
qui est-ce qui est là? ⎭ *who is there?*

qui avez-vous rencontré? *who(m) did you*
qui est-ce que vous avez *meet?*
rencontré?

AFTER PREPOSITIONS:
à qui avez-vous donné la lettre?
to whom did you give the letter?
à qui est ce stylo? *whose pen is this?*
de qui parlais-tu? *who were you talking about?*
de qui est-il l'ami? *whose friend is he?*
avec qui joue-t-elle? *who does she play with?*

♦ **qu'est-ce qui, qu'est-ce que, que** *what?*
qu'est-ce qui se passe? *what is happening?*
que* faites-vous? ⎫
qu'est-ce que* vous faites? ⎭ *what are you doing?*
*****que** becomes **qu'** before a vowel:
qu'a-t-il dit?/qu'est-ce qu'il a dit? *what did he say?*

♦ **quoi** (*after a preposition: what?*)
à quoi penses-tu? *what are you thinking about?*
de quoi parlaient-ils? *what were they talking about?*

♦ **quel, quelle, quels, quelles** *what/which...?*

The French equivalent of the interrogative adjectives
'what' and 'which' has four forms:
quel   +masculine singular noun
quelle +feminine singular noun
quels   +masculine plural noun
quelles +feminine plural noun

e.g. **quel** est son **nom**? *what is his name?*
quelle raison a-t-elle donnée? *what reason did she give?*
quels pays avez-vous visités? *what(which)*

countries have you visited?
quelles matières étudiez-vous? *what (which) subjects are you taking?*

◆ **lequel, laquelle, lesquels, lesquelles** *which?, which one(s)?*

The French equivalent of the interrogative pronoun 'which (one)' has four forms:
lequel refers to a masculine singular noun
laquelle refers to a feminine singular noun
lesquels refers to a masculine plural noun
lesquelles refers to a feminine plural noun

(le livre) > **lequel** préférez-vous?
which one do you prefer?
(la bague) > **laquelle** portait-elle?
which one was she wearing?
(les livres) > **lesquels** lis-tu?
which ones are you reading?
(les photos) > **lesquelles** aimez-vous?
which ones do you like?

These pronouns can refer to people as well as to things:
lequel/laquelle d'entre vous a ouvert les fenêtres?
lesquels/lesquelles d'entre vous ont ouvert les fenêtres?
which of you opened the windows?

POINTS TO NOTE:

1. After **à** (*at/to*): à+lequel=**auquel**
   à+lesquels=**auxquels**
   à+lesquelles=**auxquelles**
   e.g. **auquel** a-t-il envoyé la lettre? *which one did he send the letter to?*

   Note: à+laquelle remains **à laquelle**

2. After **de** (*of*): de+lequel=**duquel**
   de+lesquels=**desquels**
   de+lesquelles=**desquelles**
   e.g. **desquels** parles-tu? *which ones are you talking about?*

   Note: de+laquelle remains **de laquelle**

102 QUI

♦ *ANSWERS TO QUESTIONS*

Oui (*yes*): Êtes-vous content? – **Oui**
Are you happy? Yes (I am)

Non (*no*): Êtes-vous content? – **Non**
Are you happy? No (I'm not)

Si (*yes*): (contradicting a negative question/statement)
Vous n'êtes pas content? – **Si**
Aren't you happy? Yes (I am)

Note: there is no straightforward equivalent in French of the 'I am, we do, he will' type of reply

qui 1. (*interrogative*) **qui a téléphoné?** *who rang?;* **à qui parles-tu?** *who are you speaking to?;* see also QUESTIONS

2. (*relative*) **la personne qui m'a parlé** *the person who spoke to me;* **les enfants avec qui il jouait** *the children he was playing with;* see also SENTENCES

quoi 1. (*what*) **il ne sait pas quoi dire** *he doesn't know what to say;* **en quoi est-ce fait?** *what is it made of?;* see also QUESTIONS

2. (*whatever*) **quoi que tu dises** *whatever you may say;* **quoi qu'il arrive** *whatever happens;* note the use of the SUBJUNCTIVE

reflexive verbs e.g. 'se laver' (to wash (oneself))

♦ 1. A reflexive verb in French is formed by a reflexive pronoun (me, te, se, nous, vous) + verb

e.g. **se laver** *to wash (oneself)*
    se lever *to get up*
    s'habiller *to dress (oneself)*

The reflexive pronoun always 'agrees' with its subject: 'il se lave' (he washes himself), 'nous nous lavons' (we wash ourselves)

The present tense of 'se laver' is:

je **me** lave	*I wash (myself)*
tu **te** laves	*you wash (yourself)*
il **se** lave	*he washes (himself)*
on **se** lave	*one washes (oneself)*

REFLEXIVE VERBS

elle **se** lave	*she washes (herself)*
nous **nous** lavons	*we wash (ourselves)*
vous **vous** lavez	*you wash (yourself/yourselves)*
ils **se** lavent	*they wash (themselves)*
elles **se** lavent	*they wash (themselves)*

Other tenses are:

IMPERFECT	je me lavais *etc*
PAST HISTORIC	je me lavai *etc*
FUTURE	je me laverai *etc*
CONDITIONAL	je me laverais *etc*

Note:

  a. 'me', 'te', 'se' become 'm'', 't'' and 's'', respectively before a vowel or an 'h' mute:

e.g. je **m'**appelle ...
    tu **t'**habilles
    il/elle **s'**ennuie
    ils/elles **s'**asseyent

  b. See section on IMPERATIVES

♦ 2. Reflexive verbs have 'être' as their auxiliary in compound tenses. The past participle of a reflexive verb 'agrees' with its direct object if that object comes before the verb, adding:

'e' if the direct object is feminine singular;
's' if the direct object is masculine plural, and
'es' if the direct object is feminine plural

e.g.

PERFECT	*PLUPERFECT*
je me suis lavé(e)	je m'étais lavé(e) *etc*
tu t'es lavé(e)	
il/elle s'est lavé(e)	*FUTURE PERFECT*
nous nous sommes lavé(e)s	je me serai lavé(e) *etc*
vous vous êtes lavé(e)/lavé(e)s	*CONDITIONAL PERFECT*
ils/elles se sont lavé(e)s	je me serais lavé(e) *etc*

♦ 3. Study the following examples:

  a. elle s'est brossé les cheveux/les dents
    she brushed her hair/her teeth
  nous nous sommes lavé les cheveux/les mains *we washed our hair/our hands*

The past participle doesn't change since the direct object – 'les cheveux', 'les dents', 'les mains' – follows the verb. The 's" and 'nous' are *indirect* objects here (literally: she brushed *to herself* the hair/teeth; we washed *to ourselves* the hair/hands)

    b. ils se sont aimés
        they loved each other/one another
    nous nous sommes écrit des lettres
        we wrote letters to each other/one another

Note that the reflexive pronoun can have the translation '(to) each other/one another'

    c. ça se répare facilement
        it is easily repaired
    ça se vend bien
        it sells well

Note that the reflexive can be used with passive value

relative pronouns see SENTENCES

rendre
1. rendre quelque chose à quelqu'un: **je lui ai rendu son livre** *I gave him his book back*

2. rendre quelqu'un malade/nerveux etc: **ça l'a rendu malade** *it made him ill*

3. se rendre quelque part: **ils se sont rendus sur les lieux de l'accident** *they went to the scene of the accident*

rester
1. (*place*) **reste-là, je reviens tout de suite!** *stay here, I'll be back in a moment*

2. (*state*) **nous sommes restés silencieux** *we remained silent*

3. (*still remaining*) **il reste 2 heures à attendre** *we've still 2 hours to wait;* **il me reste très peu d'argent** *I've very little money left;* **il restait un peu de lait** *there was a little milk left*

rien
1. **je n'ai rien vu** *I didn't see anything;* **rien n'a changé** *nothing has changed;* see also NEGATIVES

2. **sans rien dire** *without saying anything*

sa see POSSESSIVES

sans 1. (*before a noun*) **sans manteau** *without a coat;* **sans père** *fatherless;* **sans manches** *sleeveless;* **sans un meuble** *without a single piece of furniture*

2. (*before a verb*) **il est parti sans dire au revoir** *he left without saying goodbye;* **il est parti sans dire un mot** *he left without saying a word;* **il l'a éteint sans s'en apercevoir** *he switched it off without noticing*

3. **sans que: il est parti sans que je m'en aperçoive** *he left without my noticing it;* note the use of the SUBJUNCTIVE (compare also with 2, where both verbs have the same subject)

savoir for conjugation see IRREGULAR VERBS

1. (*to know something*) **je sais son adresse** *I know his address;* **je sais qu'il habite à Londres** *I know he lives in London;* **je ne savais pas qu'il était rentré** *I didn't know he was back*

2. (*to know how*) **il ne sait pas nager** *he can't swim*

3. **faire savoir: faites-moi savoir quand vous serez prêt** *let me know when you are ready.*

se 1. (*himself, herself, oneself*) **il se lave** *he washes (himself);* **ou peut se tromper** *everybody can make a mistake;* **allez, on se dépêche!** *come on, let's hurry up!*

2. (*each other*) **ils se ressemblent** *they resemble each other*

see also REFLEXIVE VERBS

3. (*passive use*) **cela se répare très facilement** *it's very easily repaired;* **ça ne se dit pas** *it isn't said*

sentences

1. Statements
   Word order is similar to English, except as regards PERSONAL PRONOUNS and when following direct speech*

je suis/content
I am /happy

le soleil/brille
the sun/is shining

nous sommes arrivés/hier
we arrived /yesterday

elle a acheté/les billets
she bought /the tickets
elle **les** a achetés
she bought them

il parle /à sa mère
he is talking/to his mother
il **lui** parle
he is talking to her

j'écris /une lettre/au directeur
I am writing/a letter /to the headmaster

je **lui** écris une lettre
I am writing him a letter
je **la lui** écris
I am writing it to him

je voudrais /essayer /cette robe
I would like/to try on/this dress
je voudrais l'essayer
I would like to try it on

* With direct speech:
    vous avez tort, dit-elle
      you are wrong, she said
    est-ce vrai? demanda Suzanne
      is it true? asked Suzanne

2. see NEGATIVES

3. see QUESTIONS

4. Commands: see IMPERATIVES

5. Combining phrases and sentences
♦ **qui; que** *who; which/that*
  SUBJECT l'homme **qui** parle
             the man who is speaking
             la porte **qui** est ouverte
             the door which is open

  OBJECT la fille **que*** vous voyez
             the girl (that) you see
             le bâtiment **que*** vous voyez
             the building (which) you see

* before a VOWEL **que** becomes **qu'**:
la femme **qu'**il a rencontrée
the woman (whom) he met
le repas **qu'**elle prépare
the meal (which) she is preparing

Note that English sometimes leaves out 'which' or 'that, whom'; French *always* includes the pronoun

SENTENCES 107

AFTER PREPOSITIONS:
e.g. les enfants **avec qui** il jouait
the children with whom he played
l'homme au fils **de qui** j'ai donné le livre
the man to whose son I gave the book

♦ **quoi** *(after a preposition: what)*
je ne sais pas **à quoi** il pense
I don't know what he's thinking about
elle m'a demandé **de quoi** ils parlaient
she asked me what they were talking about

♦ **lequel, laquelle, lesquels, lesquelles** *(after preposition: which)*

lequel	refers to a masculine singular noun
laquelle	refers to a feminine singular noun
lesquels	refers to a masculine plural noun
lesquelles	refers to a feminine plural noun

e.g. le stylo avec **lequel** il écrivait
the pen he was writing with
la boîte dans **laquelle** il l'a mis
the box he put it in
les champs vers **lesquels** il courait
the fields towards which he was running
les nuits pendant **lesquelles** il travaillait
the nights during which he worked

Points to note:
(a) à+lequel=**auquel**
à+lesquels=**auxquels**
à+lesquelles=**auxquelles**

e.g. le club **auquel** il appartient
the club he belongs to
les adresses **auxquelles** j'écris
the addresses to which I'm writing

(b) de+lequel=**duquel**
de+lesquels=**desquels**
de+lesquelles=**desquelles**

e.g. le film **duquel** il parlait
the film he was talking about

Note: laquelle does not contract with à/de: **à laquelle, de laquelle**

108 SES

♦ **ce qui, ce que, ce dont** *what*
je ne sais pas **ce qui** se passe
I don't know what is happening
ce qui m'agace c'est que...
what annoys me is that...

elle ne comprend pas **ce que*** vous dites
she doesn't understand what you say
ce que* nous avons fait, c'était...
what we did was...

ce dont il parle ne m'intéresse pas
what he's talking about doesn't interest me
donne-lui **ce dont** il a besoin
give him what he needs

* **ce que** becomes **ce qu'** before a vowel:
savez-vous ce qu'il veut dire?
do you know what he means?

Note: **tout** { **ce qui** / **ce que** } = *all that, everything that:*

e.g. c'est tout ce qu'il a dit
that's all he said
c'est tout ce que je veux
that's all I want

ses see POSSESSIVES

si 1. (*if, whether*) **si** vous voulez partir *if you want to go;* je ne sais pas **s'il** est là *I don't know whether he's in;* **s'il** veut y aller, et **qu'il** fait beau... *if he wants to go and the weather is fine...;* note the use of 'que' after 'et' introducing a second hypothesis

2. (*so, such*) il était **si** malade que... *he was so ill that...;* une **si** belle auto *such a beautiful car*

3. (*after negative question*) vous ne venez pas? — **si**, j'arrive *aren't you coming? — yes I am;* vous n'en voulez pas? — mais **si**! *don't you want any? — of course I do!*

sien, son *etc* see POSSESSIVES

soi 1. (*impersonal: himself/herself*) ne penser

qu'à soi *to think only about oneself*; si on n'agit que pour soi *if one is only acting for oneself*; avoir un peu d'argent sur soi *to have a little cash on one*
2. cela va de soi *that goes without saying*
3. soi-même *oneself*

subjunctive

The present subjunctive of regular verbs is formed as follows:

DONNER	FINIR	VENDRE
je donne	je finisse	je vende
tu donnes	tu finisses	tu vendes
il/elle donne	il/elle finisse	il/elle vende
nous donnions	nous finissions	nous vendions
vous donniez	vous finissiez	vous vendiez
ils/elles donnent	ils/elles finissent	ils/elles vendent

'avoir' and 'être' are irregular:

AVOIR	ÊTRE
j'aie	je sois
tu aies	tu sois
il/elle ait	il/elle soit
nous ayons	nous soyons
vous ayez	vous soyez
ils/elles aient	ils/elles soient

The main uses of the subjunctive are:
1. after **bien que** ⎫
      quoique ⎬ *although*
      pour que ⎫
      afin que ⎬ *so that*
      jusqu'à ce que *until*
      il faut que: il faut que vous partiez
      you must leave, you'll have to leave
   e.g. bien qu'il **soit** malade
      although he's ill
      afin qu'il ne m'**entende** pas
      so that he doesn't hear me
2. after verbs of wishing/fearing:
   voulez-vous que je **parte**?
   do you want me to leave?
   il craint que vous ne l'**aimiez** pas
   he's afraid you don't love him

SUPERLATIVE

3. after other verbs of emotion:
   avoir honte que... *to be ashamed that*...
   être content que... *to be pleased that*...
   regretter que... *to be sorry that*...
4. after verbs of saying and thinking (when uncertainty involved):
   je ne pense pas qu'il **vienne**
   I don't think he'll come/he's coming
5. after a superlative:
   c'est la plus belle ville que j'**aie** jamais vue
   it's the most beautiful town I've ever seen

superlative see COMPARATIVE

ta see POSSESSIVES

tant 1. (*so much*) **il parle tant** *he talks so much*
   2. **tant de**...: **il boit tant de vin que**... *he drinks so much wine that*...; **il lit tant de livres que**... *he reads so many books that*...; **il a montré tant de patience** *he has shown such patience*
   3. **tant que: restez à la maison tant qu'il pleuvra** *stay inside while it's raining;* note the difference in the use of tenses

te see PERSONAL PRONOUNS

tellement 1. (*so much*) **il a tellement plu** *it's been raining so much*
   2. (*so*) **je suis tellement fatigué** *I'm so very tired*
   3. **tellement de: il y a tellement de monde** *there are so many people;* **il a perdu tellement de temps** *he has wasted so much time;* **il y en a tellement que nous ne savons plus qu'en faire** *there are so many we don't know what to do with them any more*

tes see POSSESSIVES

tenir for conjugation see IRREGULAR VERBS
   1. (*to hold*) **il tenait un livre à la main** *he was holding a book in his hand*
   2. (*care about*) **tenir à: je tiens à ce livre** *I treasure this book;* **je tiens à ce que ce soit fait rapidement** *I do want this to be done quickly*

3. se tenir: se tenir debout *to be standing;* **tiens-toi droit** *stand up straight;* **elle se tient très mal** *she behaves very badly*

tenses   Use of tenses (for formation see VERB FORMS)

1. *Present*

   Used in a way similar to English. The main difference to note is that French has no separate equivalent of the English '-ing' form, as in 'I am work*ing*':

il **regarde** la télévision	*he is watching television*
il **commence** à pleuvoir	*it is starting to rain*
je **pars** demain	*I'm leaving tomorrow*
je **me lève** à 7 heures du matin	*I get up at 7 a.m.*
elle **habite** à Paris	*she lives in Paris*

2. *Imperfect*

   Used to describe:

   (i) an action or state in the past without definite limits in time:

   nous **sortions** quand il est arrivé
   we were leaving when he arrived
   (i.e. we were in the process of leaving but had not yet left)

   elle **portait** une robe bleue
   she wore/was wearing a blue dress

   le soleil **brillait**
   the sun shone/was shining

   (ii) habitual actions in the past:

   je **prenais** le train de 7h.30
   I caught   the 7.30 train
     used to catch
     would catch

   elle **nageait** tous les jours
   she swam   every day
     used to swim
     would swim

   See also DEPUIS, FAIRE, IL Y A

3. *Perfect*
   Used to describe a completed action in the past:
   j'**ai ouvert** les fenêtres
   I opened/have opened the windows

   elle **a perdu** son porte-monnaie
   she lost/has lost her purse

   Note: the perfect is the tense used in conversation and in letter-writing

4. *Past Historic*
   The past historic is a literary form, referring to single completed events in the past It is never used in conversation.

5. *Future*
   Used largely as in English:
   il **sera** content *he will be pleased*
   je **lirai** un livre *I will read a book*

   Note however:
   (a) After **quand** (*when*) French uses the future or future perfect where English generally uses the present or the perfect:

   dites-le-lui quand vous le **verrez**
   tell him when you see him
   nous partirons quand nous l'**aurons fait**
   we will leave when we've done it

   (b) The 'futur immédiat' – **aller** + infinitive – is used for actions or events just about to happen:
   je vais manquer le train
   I'll miss or *I'm going to miss the train*
   il va le faire demain
   he'll do it or *he's going to do it tomorrow*
   il allait le faire
   he was about to do it

6. *Conditional*
   Used largely as in English:
   il **serait** content *he would be pleased*
   je **lirais** un livre *I would read a book*

tien *etc* see POSSESSIVES

TIME 113

time

(it's) 2.00	(il est) deux heures
2.05	deux heures cinq
2.10	deux heures dix
2.15	deux heures et quart
2.20	deux heures vingt
2.25	deux heures vingt-cinq
2.30	deux heures et demie
2.35	trois heures moins vingt-cinq
2.40	trois heures moins vingt
2.45	trois heures moins le quart
2.50	trois heures moins dix
2.55	trois heures moins cinq
3.00	trois heures
12.00	midi
12.30	midi et demi
24.00	minuit
00.30	minuit et demi

Note:

2.00 – 2.30: minutes and the quarter-/half-hour are *added* to the hour

2.35 – 2.55: minutes and the quarter-hour are *subtracted* (**moins**=minus, less) from the next hour

♦ a.m. or p.m.?

French distinguishes a.m. from p.m. in two ways:

i) by adding:
   du matin *(in the morning)*
   de l'après-midi *(in the afternoon)*
   du soir *(in the evening)*
   e.g. **cinq heures du matin/de l'après-midi**
     5 a.m./p.m.
   onze heures du soir *11 p.m.*

ii) by using the 24 hour clock:
   01.10 une heure dix (1.10 a.m.)
   13.10 treize heures dix (1.10 p.m.)
   14.15 quatorze heures quinze (2.15 p.m.)
   19.30 dix-neuf heures trente (7.30 p.m.)

   Remember that **midi**=12 a.m. or noon
           minuit=12 p.m. or midnight

♦ Some useful vocabulary:
quelle heure est-il? – il est . . .
what time is it? – It's . . .
à quelle heure est-ce que vous arrivez? – **à une heure et demie** — *what time are you arriving? – half past one*
avez-vous l'heure? *have you got the time?*
au bout de vingt minutes *after twenty minutes*
vers huit heures *around eight o'clock*
à sept heures **précises** *at seven o'clock sharp*
dans un quart d'heure/une demi-heure *in a quarter of an hour/half an hour*
ma montre **avance/retarde de** dix minutes *my watch is ten minutes fast/slow*
nous avons trois heures **de retard** *we are three hours late*
le train **de** cinq heures *the five o'clock train*
elle est partie **il y a** cinq minutes *she left five minutes ago*
la pièce **dure** deux heures *the play lasts (for) two hours*

ton see POSSESSIVES

tout, tous 1. (*adjective*) **il a bu tout le café** *he drank all the coffee;* **il a plu toute la journée** *it rained the whole day;* **tous les jours** *every day*

2. (*pronoun*) **je les connais tous/toutes** *I know them all;* **tout est prêt** *everything is ready*

3. **tout le monde** *everybody*

4. **tout ce qui, tout ce que: tout ce qui est arrivé** *everything that happened;* **tout ce qu'il possède** *everything (that) he owns;* **fais tout ce que tu veux** *do whatever you want;* see also SENTENCES

5. **tout de suite** *immediately*

très 1. (*very*) **il faisait très froid** *it was very cold;* **il était très fâché** *he was very angry;* **il avait très faim** *he was very hungry*

2. **très peu: il a très peu de temps/d'amis** *he has very little time/very few friends*

trop 1. **trop de . . .** (*too many, too much*); **il y a**

trop de monde *there are too many people;* **il y a trop de bruit** *there's too much noise;* **il y a trop d'erreurs** *there are too many mistakes*

2. (*too*) **c'est trop loin** *it's too far;* **c'est trop cher** *it's too expensive*

3. (*too much*) **nous avons trop mangé** *we've eaten too much*

4. **de trop: tu m'as donné 2 francs de trop** *you've given me 2 francs too much*

tu see PERSONAL PRONOUNS

un, une see ARTICLES

valoir for conjugation see IRREGULAR VERBS
  1. (*to be worth*) **ça vaut 5 francs** *it's worth 5 francs;* **ça ne vaut rien du tout** *it's worth nothing at all*
  2. (*to be equivalent to*) **ce dictionnaire vaut bien celui-là** *this dictionary is as good as that one*
  3. (*impersonal*) **valoir mieux: il vaut mieux partir maintenant** *it's better to leave now*
  4. **valoir la peine: ça vaut la peine d'être vu** *it's worth seeing.*

venir for conjugation see IRREGULAR VERBS
  (*as an auxiliary: for recent past*) **venir de faire: je viens de lire un bon roman** *I've just read a good novel;* **il venait de partir** *he had just left;* see also ALLER

verbal constructions

1. There are three main constructions:

A) verb+infinitive: **il espère venir**
    he is hoping to come
B) verb+**de**+infinitive: **il a décidé de venir**
    he has decided to come
C) verb+**à**+infinitive: **il a réussi à venir**
    he managed to come

Some of the most common examples of these constructions are:

A) **devoir faire** *to have to do*
   falloir faire *to have to do*

VERBAL CONSTRUCTIONS

pouvoir faire *to be able to do*
savoir faire *to know how to do*
vouloir faire *to want to do*
aimer (bien) faire *to like to do/doing*
aimer mieux faire *to prefer to do/doing*
compter faire *to expect to do*
désirer faire *to want to do*
espérer faire *to hope to do*
oser faire *to dare (to) do*
préférer faire *to prefer to do*
sembler faire *to seem to do*

aller/venir/descendre *etc* **faire** *to go/come/go down etc to do*

e.g. il est allé la rencontrer *he has gone to meet her*
venez voir *come and see*

Notes
1) je veux **partir** *I want to leave*
   je veux **qu'il parte** *I want him to leave*
   il préfère **rester** *he prefers to stay*
   il préfère **que vous restiez** *he prefers you to stay*

   The infinitive after verbs of wishing etc cannot be used when there is a change of subject: **'que'** + subjunctive is used instead.
2) After verbs of seeing and hearing (i.e. **'voir'** (*to see*); **'regarder'** (*to watch*); **'apercevoir'** (*to see*); **'entendre'** (*to hear*); **'écouter'** (*to listen to*)), the infinitive is used:

   elle a vu sortir son mari *she saw her husband come out*

   il les entendait parler *he heard them talking*

   Note the word order in French
3) **faire faire ...** *to have ... done; to make ... do*
   e.g. il a fait monter ses bagages *he had his luggage taken up*
   le film l'a fait pleurer *the film made her cry*

   set expressions
   faire venir quelqu'un *to send for somebody:*
   elle a fait venir le médecin *she sent for the doctor*
   faire entrer quelqu'un *to show somebody in:*
   faites-les entrer *show them in*

VERBAL CONSTRUCTIONS 117

4) **j'ai failli tomber** *I almost fell*
5) **laisser faire** *to let ... do/allow ... to do:*
   laissez-moi finir *let me finish*
6) **laisser tomber** *to drop:*
   elle a laissé tomber son couteau *she dropped her knife*
7) **aller chercher** *to go for, fetch:*
   va les chercher *go and get them*
8) **envoyer chercher** *to send for:*
   ils ont envoyé chercher un prêtre *they sent for a priest*

B) **s'arrêter de faire** *to stop doing*
   cesser de faire *to stop doing*
   commencer de faire *to begin to do*
   craindre de faire *to be afraid of doing*
   décider de faire *to decide to do*
   se dépêcher de faire *to hurry to do*
   essayer de faire *to try to do*
   éviter de faire *to avoid doing*
   s'excuser de faire *to apologize for doing*
   finir de faire *to finish doing; to stop doing*
   jurer de faire *to swear to do*
   menacer de faire *to threaten to do*
   offrir de faire *to offer to do*
   oublier de faire *to forget to do*
   proposer de faire *to suggest doing*
   refuser de faire *to refuse to do*
   regretter de faire/d'avoir fait *to regret doing/having done*
   se souvenir d'avoir fait *to remember doing/having done*
   tenter de faire *to try to do*
   venir de faire *to have just done*

C) **apprendre à faire** *to learn to do*
   s'attendre à faire *to expect to do*
   chercher à faire *to try to do*
   commencer à faire *to begin to do*
   consentir à faire *to agree to do*
   se décider à faire *to decide to do*
   s'habituer à faire *to get used to doing*

118 VERBAL CONSTRUCTIONS

hésiter à faire *to hesitate to do*
s'intéresser à faire *to be interested in doing*
se mettre à faire *to begin to do*
penser à faire *to think of doing*
se préparer à faire *to get ready to do*
réussir à faire *to succeed in doing*
songer à faire *to think about doing*

2. In the following constructions, 'quelqu'un' (*somebody*) is shortened to 'qn' (*sb*).

i) **accuser qn d'avoir fait*** *to accuse sb of doing/having done*
blâmer qn d'avoir fait* *to blame sb for doing/having done*
dissuader qn de faire *to dissuade sb from doing*
empêcher qn de faire *to prevent sb from doing*
féliciter qn d'avoir fait* *to congratulate sb on doing/having done*
persuader qn de faire *to persuade sb to do*
prier qn de faire *to ask sb to do*
remercier qn d'avoir fait* *to thank sb for doing/having done*

aider qn à faire *to help sb to do*
encourager qn à faire *to encourage sb to do*
forcer qn à faire *to force sb to do*
inviter qn à faire *to invite sb to do*
obliger qn à faire *to force sb to do*
pousser qn à faire *to urge sb to do*

ii) **conseiller à qn de faire** *to advise sb to do*
défendre à qn de faire *to forbid sb to do*
demander à qn de faire *to ask sb to do*
dire à qn de faire *to tell sb to do*
interdire à qn de faire *to forbid sb to do*
ordonner à qn de faire *to order sb to do*
pardonner à qn d'avoir fait *to forgive sb for doing/having done*
permettre à qn de faire *to allow sb to do*
promettre à qn de faire *to promise sb to do*

iii) **apprendre à qn à faire** *to teach sb to do*

3. a) The infinitive also follows:
  i) certain prepositions:
    pour (*to*):
    il l'a fait pour l'effrayer
    he did it to frighten her
    sans (*without*):
    il est entré sans frapper
    he came in without knocking
    avant de (*before*):
    venez me voir avant de partir
    come and see me before you leave
    au lieu de (*instead of*):
    elle est partie au lieu d'attendre
    she left instead of waiting

  ii) certain verbal constructions:
  e.g. **avoir peur de** (*to be afraid of*):
    il a peur de la blesser
    he's afraid of hurting her
    avoir honte de (*to be ashamed of*):
    elle a honte de mentir
    she's ashamed of lying
    faire semblant de (*to pretend to*):
    il faisait semblant de lire
    he was pretending to read

  iii) nouns and adjectives:
    un moyen de le faire *a way of doing it*
    avoir l'occasion de faire *to have the opportunity to do*

    prêt à faire *ready to do*
    content de faire *pleased to do*

b) The perfect infinitive (**avoir** or **être**+past participle) follows the preposition 'après' (*after*):
    après avoir mangé, il ...
    after eating, he ...
    après être partie, elle ...
    after leaving, she ...
    après nous être lavés, nous ...
    after washing, we ...

verb forms
♦ *SIMPLE TENSES*

Below are the patterns for regular verbs whose infinitives end in '-er', '-ir', or '-re': e.g. donn**er**; fin**ir**; vend**re**. See also IRREGULAR VERBS

The tenses shown are:
1. *Present:* e.g. je **vends** *I am selling*
   I sell
2. *Imperfect:* e.g. je **vendais** *I was selling*
   I sold
3. *Past Historic:* e.g. je **vendis** *I sold*
4. *Future:* e.g. je **vendrai** *I will sell*
5. *Conditional:* e.g. je **vendrais** *I would sell*

Also shown are: a. *Past participle*
b. *Present participle*
c. *Imperative* (i.e. command form): for formation see IMPERATIVES.

Each of the tenses is formed by a stem + ending, the ending varying according to the subject pronoun (see PERSONAL PRONOUNS) and the verb type to which the infinitive belongs.

A. '-er' verb: donner (*to give*)

For the present imperfect and past historic tenses take off the '-er' and add the ending:

	PRESENT	IMPERFECT	PAST HISTORIC
je	donne	donnais	donnai
tu	donnes	donnais	donnas
il/elle/on	donne	donnait	donna
nous	donn**ons**	donn**ions**	donn**âmes**
vous	donn**ez**	donn**iez**	donn**âtes**
ils/elles	donn**ent**	donn**aient**	donn**èrent**

For the future and conditional tenses add the ending to the infinitive:

	FUTURE	CONDITIONAL
je	donner**ai**	donner**ais**
tu	donner**as**	donner**ais**
il/elle/on	donner**a**	donner**ait**
nous	donner**ons**	donner**ions**

vous	donne**rez**	donne**riez**
ils/elles	donne**ront**	donne**raient**

Past participle: take off '-er' and add 'é': donn**é**
Present participle: take off '-er' and add '**ant**': donn**ant**
Imperative: donne
            donnons
            donnez

Points to note
The spelling of some '**-er**' verbs changes when certain endings are added. Below we give you the ones you will have to remember.

1. '**-cer**': c > ç before a, o
   e.g. lancer (*to throw*) PRESENT PARTICIPLE lançant

PRESENT	IMPERFECT	PAST HISTORIC
nous lançons	je lançais	je lançai
	tu lançais	tu lanças
	il/elle lançait	il/elle lança
	ils/elles lançaient	nous lançâmes
		vous lançâtes

2. '**-ger**': g > ge before a, o
   e.g. manger (*to eat*) PRESENT PARTICIPLE mangeant

PRESENT	IMPERFECT	PAST HISTORIC
nous mangeons	je mangeais	je mangeai
	tu mangeais	tu mangeas
	il/elle mangeait	il/elle mangea
	ils/elle mangeaient	nous mangeâmes
		vous mangeâtes

3. a) '**-eler**'
   (i) l > ll before 'e', 'es', 'ent' in the present tense, and in the future and conditional
   e.g. appeler (*to call*)

PRESENT	FUTURE	CONDITIONAL
j'appelle	j'appellerai	j'appellerais
tu appelles	*etc*	*etc*
il/elle appelle		
ils/elles appellent		

(ii) e.g. **peler, geler** *etc*: see 4.
b) '**-eter**'
(i) **t > tt** before 'e', 'es', 'ent' in the present tense, and in the future and conditional
e.g. jeter (*to throw*)

PRESENT	*FUTURE*	*CONDITIONAL*
je jette	je jetterai	je jetterais
tu jettes	*etc*	*etc*
il/elle jette		
ils/elles jettent		

(ii) e.g. **acheter**: see 4.

4. '**-e+consonant+er**': **e > è** before consonant+'e', 'es', 'ent' in the present tense, and in the future and conditional
e.g. mener (*to lead*)

PRESENT	*FUTURE*	*CONDITIONAL*
je mène	je mènerai	je mènerais
tu mènes	*etc*	*etc*
il/elle mène		
ils/elles mènent		

5. '**-é+consonant+er**': **é > è** before consonant+'e', 'es', 'ent' in the present tense
e.g. préférer (*to prefer*)

PRESENT
je préfère
tu préfères
il/elle préfère
ils/elles préfèrent

6. '**-yer**': **y > i** before 'e', 'es', 'ent' in the present tense, and in the future and conditional
e.g. nettoyer (*to clean*)

PRESENT	*FUTURE*	*CONDITIONAL*
je nettoie	je nettoierai	je nettoierais
tu nettoies	*etc*	*etc*
il/elle nettoie		
ils/elles nettoient		

B. '**-ir**' verb: **finir** (*to finish*)
For the present, imperfect and past historic tenses, take off the '**-ir**' and add the ending:

	PRESENT	IMPERFECT	PAST HISTORIC
je	finis	finissais	finis
tu	finis	finissais	finis
il/elle/on	finit	finissait	finit
nous	finissons	finissions	finîmes
vous	finissez	finissiez	finîtes
ils/elles	finissent	finissaient	finirent

For the future and conditional tenses, add the ending to the infinitive:

	FUTURE	CONDITIONAL
je	finirai	finirais
tu	finiras	finirais
il/elle/on	finira	finirait
nous	finirons	finirions
vous	finirez	finiriez
ils/elles	finiront	finiraient

Past participle: take off '**-ir**' and add '**-i**': fini
Present participle: take off '**-ir**' and add '**-issant**': fin**issant**
Imperative: finis
　　　　　　finissons
　　　　　　finissez

C. '-re' verb: **vendre** (*to sell*)

For the present, imperfect and past historic tenses, take off the '**-re**' and add the ending:

	PRESENT	IMPERFECT	PAST HISTORIC
je	vends	vendais	vendis
tu	vends	vendais	vendis
il/elle/on	vend	vendait	vendit
nous	vendons	vendions	vendîmes
vous	vendez	vendiez	vendîtes
ils/elles	vendent	vendaient	vendirent

For the future and conditional tenses, take off the '**-e**' and add the ending:

	FUTURE	CONDITIONAL
je	vendrai	vendrais
tu	vendras	vendrais

124 VERB FORMS

il/elle/on	vend**ra**	vend**rait**
nous	vend**rons**	vend**rions**
vous	vend**rez**	vend**riez**
ils/elles	vend**ront**	vend**raient**

Past participle: take off '-**re**' and add '-**u**': vend**u**
Present participle: take off '-**re**' and add '-**ant**': vend**ant**
Imperative: vends
           vendons
           vendez

♦ *COMPOUND TENSES*

These are formed by an auxiliary verb (**avoir** or **être**, see IRREGULAR VERBS) plus a past participle.

To form the past participle of a regular verb:
take off the '-**er**' ending and add '-**é**': donner: donné
take off the '-**ir**' ending and add '-**i**': finir: fini
take off the '-**re**' ending and add '-**u**': vendre: vendu

The compound tenses are:

1. *Perfect:* formed by the **present** tense of the auxiliary verb + past participle
   e.g. j'**ai** vendu   *I have sold*
                         I sold
       je **suis** allé   *I have gone*
                         I went

2. *Pluperfect:* formed by the **imperfect** tense of the auxiliary verb + past participle
   e.g. j'**avais** vendu   *I had sold*
       j'**étais** allé   *I had gone*

3. *Future Perfect:* formed by the **future** tense of the auxiliary verb + past participle
   e.g. j'**aurai** vendu   *I will have sold*
       je **serai** allé   *I will have gone*

4. *Conditional Perfect:* formed by the **conditional** tense of the auxiliary verb + past participle
   e.g. j'**aurais** vendu   *I would have sold*
       je **serais** allé   *I would have gone*

Thus, the compound tenses of 'vendre' are:

PERFECT	PLUPERFECT
j'ai vendu	j'avais vendu

tu as vendu
il/elle/on a vendu
nous avons vendu
vous avez vendu
ils/elles ont vendu

tu avais vendu
il/elle/on avait vendu
nous avions vendu
vous aviez vendu
ils/elles avaient vendu

FUTURE PERFECT
j'aurai vendu
tu auras vendu
il/elle/on aura vendu
nous aurons vendu
vous aurez vendu
ils/elles auront vendu

CONDITIONAL PERFECT
j'aurais vendu
tu aurais vendu
il/elle/on aurait vendu
nous aurions vendu
vous auriez vendu
ils/elles auraient vendu

♦ *auxiliary and agreement*
Most verbs take the auxiliary **avoir** to form their compound tenses. Of the few which take **être** the most common (all intransitive) are:

arriver *to arrive, to happen*
partir *to leave*
entrer *to go/come in*
sortir *to go/come out*
aller *to go*
venir *to come*
devenir *to become*
passer *to pass (by)*

monter *to go up*
descendre *to go down*
naître *to be born*
mourir *to die*
rester *to remain*
tomber *to fall*
rentrer *to go/come back*
retourner *to return*

The past participle of a verb with 'être' as its auxiliary 'agrees' with its subject*:

e.g. **aller** (*to go*): *past participle*: allé
il est allé: subject=masculine singular: past participle unchanged
elle est allée: subject=feminine singular: past participle+**e**
ils sont allés: subject=masculine plural: past participle+**s**
elles sont allées: subject=feminine plural: past participle+**es**

*See also REFLEXIVE VERBS.

Thus, the compound tenses of 'aller' with the feminine agreement shown in brackets are:

PERFECT
je suis allé(e)
tu es allé(e)
il/elle est allé(e)
nous sommes allé(e)s
vous êtes allé(e)
        allé(e)s
ils/elles sont allé(e)s

PLUPERFECT
j'étais allé(e)
tu étais allé(e)
il/elle était allé(e)
nous étions allé(e)s
vous étiez allé(e)
        allé(e)s
ils/elles étaient allé(e)s

FUTURE PERFECT
je serai allé(e)
tu seras allé(e)
il/elle sera allé(e)
nous serons allé(e)s
vous serez allé(e)
        allé(e)s
ils/elles seront allé(e)s

CONDITIONAL PERFECT
je serais allé(e)
tu serais allé(e)
il/elle serait allé(e)
nous serions allé(e)s
vous seriez allé(e)
        allé(e)s
ils/elles seraient allé(e)s

Note that two separate forms are shown for 'vous', since 'vous' can be *either* singular *or* plural (see PERSONAL PRONOUNS).

Remember that, unlike verbs which have 'être' as their auxiliary, the past participle of a verb with 'avoir' as its auxiliary does not change: (i) below. But when a verb with 'avoir' as its auxiliary has a *direct object* coming *before* it, the past participle 'agrees' with that object: (ii) below:

(i)	(ii)
elle a lu le livre	elle **l'**a lu
nous avons perdu la clef	nous **l'**avons perdue
il a fini les examens	il **les** a finis
j'ai envoyé les lettres	je **les** ai envoyées

Note that the direct object may be a phrase as well as a pronoun:

la clef que nous avons perdue *the key we lost*
celle que nous avons perdue *the one we lost*
quelles lettres ai-je envoyées? *which letters did I send?*
lesquels a-t-il finis? *which ones has he finished?*

voici 1. (*indicating*) **voici du chocolat** *here is* *some chocolate;* **voici Madame Duval** *this is Mrs Duval*

2. *(exclamation)* **le voici!** *here he is!;* **les voici!** *here they are!*

See also VOILÀ

voilà 1. *(indicating)* **voilà mon frère** *this is my brother*

2. *(exclamation)* **la voilà!** *there she is!, here she is!;* **les voilà!** *there they are!, here they are!;* **voilà** *here you are; that's it*

3. *(period of time)* **voilà une semaine que je l'attends** *that's a week that I've been waiting for him;* **voilà une année que je ne les ai pas vus** *it's a year since I last saw them;* see also DEPUIS, FAIRE, IL Y A

4. **voilà pourquoi c'est impossible** *that's why it's impossible*

Note that 'voilà' is often used for VOICI

voir for conjugation see IRREGULAR VERBS

(to see) 1. **faire voir: fais(-moi) voir ce que tu as fait** *show me what you've done*

2. *(passive sense)* **ils se sont vus refuser l'entrée** *they were turned away at the door;* **la tache se voit** *the mark is visible;* **ça se voit de loin** *you can see it from far away*

vos, votre *etc* see POSSESSIVES

vouloir for conjugation see IRREGULAR VERBS

1. *(want)* **je veux dormir** *I want to sleep;* **je veux que tu travailles** *I want you to work;* note the use of the SUBJUNCTIVE after 'vouloir que ...'

2. **vouloir dire: qu'est-ce que ça veut dire?** *what does it mean?*

3. **en vouloir à quelqu'un: il m'en veut énormément** *he has a deep grudge against me*

4. *(in the conditional tense)* **je voudrais un café** *I would like a cup of coffee;* **il aurait voulu rester** *he would have liked to stay*

vous see PERSONAL PRONOUNS

y **1.** (*as a relative pronoun: on it, in it etc*)
comment est-il entré dans la maison? > comment y est-il entré?
how did he get into the house? > how did he get into it?
je vais à Paris demain > j'y vais demain
I'm going to Paris tomorrow > I'm going there tomorrow

2. (*it, them: corresponds to a prepositional construction with 'à', compare* EN)
je pense souvent à ce problème > j'y pense souvent
I often think of this problem > I often think of it
goûtez à ces bonbons > goûtez-y
taste these sweets > taste them
ne touchez pas à ces champignons > n'y touchez pas
don't touch these mushrooms > don't touch them

3. que voulez-vous que j'y fasse? *what do you expect me to do about it?*; **je n'y peux rien** *I can't do anything about it.*

4. ça y est! *that's it!*